D0871773

DIARY *of* RUTH ANNA HATCH

EDITED *by*

MARY LOU SMITH

PUBLISHED *by the*

WOODS HOLE HISTORICAL COLLECTION

DIARY *of* RUTH ANNA HATCH

1881

© 1992 by the
Woods Hole Historical Collection
Woods Hole, Massachusetts

ISBN 0-9611374-3-6

Designed by Diane Jaroch
Rockford, Illinois

Typeset by Linda Johnson
Johnson Desktop Publishing
Rockford, Illinois

Portrait on title page:
Ruth Anna Hatch when she
wrote her Woods Hole diary in
1881, at the age of sixteen.
Courtesy Ellen Christian Keogh.

Grateful thanks to:

Donald Bourne
The Bourne Archives
Bruce Chalmers
Charlotte Christian
Bobbi Clark
William Dunkle
Mary Shiverick Fishler
Jennifer Gaines
Diane Jaroch
Ellen Christian Keogh
Jane McLaughlin
Charlotte Price
Paul Ferris Smith
Judith G. Stetson

Introduction

Ruth Anna Hatch grew up in Woods Hole, the daughter of Charles E. and Adaline Weeks Sanford Hatch. She represents a unique link in a continuing chain of generations extending back to the first Indian land purchase and forward to the present village. When she married Asa Frank Shiverick in 1891, two long-established Cape Cod families were joined. Ruth Anna lived near the north-western corner of Little Harbor in a house still standing across from the town beach next to the Coast Guard base. The piazza which she describes being rebuilt is still there and the house is still yellow with green trim.

A panoramic view of Little Harbor Courtesy WHHC..

Her father was an early commuter to Boston, riding back and forth on the train from his home in Woods Hole to his store in Boston. Her mother took in boarders. Ruth Anna began her diary on January 1, 1881, and we follow her daily life that year until she leaves Woods Hole to attend Abbot Academy in Andover, Massachusetts.

The diary disappeared from view for almost a century and survived only by extraordinary good luck; it was discovered in an abandoned local dump in 1980. The Bourne Archives, to which it was given, has generously allowed us to reprint the diary so that readers may share this wonderfully intimate view of Woods Hole as seen by a sixteen year old girl growing up on Juniper Point in 1881.

To enhance the diary, the Woods Hole Historical Collection has added photographs, many taken by Baldwin Coolidge in the late 19th Century, and editorial notes, to clarify some of the names and places mentioned in the diary. By another stroke of good luck, the sketchbook of Ruth Anna's teacher, Eva March Tappan, was in the archives of the Woods Hole Historical Collection. Miss Tappan, teacher, artist and friend of Ruth Anna, sketched the scenes of skating, sledding, walking, sailing and picking wildflowers - many of the same scenes described on the same days by Ruth Anna in her diary. Combining the photographs and sketches with the diary has added luster to those bygone days from January through September, 1881. What good days they were!

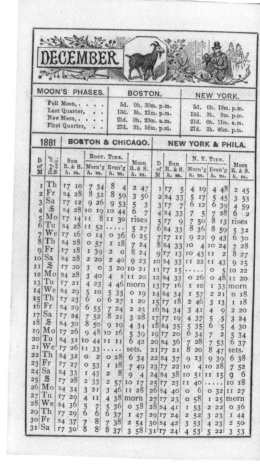

First page of Ruth Anna Hatch's diary shown here at the same size as the original. Astronomical and tide tables for Boston and New York. Courtesy Bourne Archives.

SATURDAY, JANUARY 1, 1881

I began the New Year by
getting up at at half past
eight o'clock. Nellie and I
had a candy scrape in the
morning. Made candy and
it would not harden so tried
on balls. Had bad luck.
Frank came and took Nell
and I sleighriding this
afternoon. It is lovely sleighing and I had a good time.
After I got home, went
to Ruth Shivericks and
stayed to supper. Papa
did not come home tonight.
Lizzie has Rheumatic fever
and Uncle Timmie at home
so Grandma is here and
Cousin Abbie is going to stayall night

I began the New Year by getting up at half past eight o'clock. Nellie and I had a candy scrape in the morning. Made candy and it would not harden so tried corn balls. Had bad luck!

Frank* came and took Nell and I sleigh riding this afternoon. It is lovely sleighing and I had a good time.

*Frank Shiverick

After I got home, went to Ruth Shiverick's and stayed to supper. Papa did not come home tonight. Lizzie has Rheumatic fever and Uncle Tim is at home so Grandma is here and Cousin Abbie is going to stay all night.

Walter O. Luscomb with his horse and buggy by the old barn on the corner of Depot and Railroad Avenues.

*Church of the Messiah, Episcopal

Barn later became James' Grill and then the Leeside. Mr. Luscomb often boarded at the Hatch house and

*Liberty Hall, now Community Hall

later married Lunette Shiverick.

It is quite pleasant. Went to Church* this morning. Stayed at home and read this afternoon. Josie spent the intermission here and Mr. Luscombe and Will Cahoon came in a few minutes this afternoon. Went down to the hall* to meeting with Isa Poor and Ruth Shiverick.

2

Dr. Rice preached about the particular young man. This sermon was not so funny as the one about narrow escapes. Fred came in after meeting.

It is still pleasant. I thought I would have some of the girls and boys in to spend the evening before Isa went home. I put a large pan of peanuts into the oven to bake and forgot them. When I went to look at them they were awfully black. Had to throw them away. Nellie* and I made some cornballs. They were very good this time. Addie* went sleighriding. It is the first time she has been out. In the evening Isa Poor and Ellie and Isie S. Grace and Ruth S. came but Anna could not and Bennie was too bashful. They said they had a very good time and they seemed to.

* *Ruth Anna's older sister, Ellen D.*

* *Ruth Anna's second sister, Addie M.*

It is quite pleasant. After breakfast, Ruth Shiverick came for me to go coasting and I went. We went on the hill back of the depot and side of Webster House.* It was about the best coasting I have ever seen in Woods Hole. Went again a little while in the afternoon. In the evening went to the society* at Beckie Davis's. Isa Poor went with me. Had a very good time. It snowed some this evening. Miss Tappan* came on the train tonight so must go to school tomorrow.

* *a hotel on Juniper Point*

* *Woods Hole Social Society - a discussion group*

* *her teacher*

New Vitriol Wks

Pacific Guano Co's Works
A. Shiverick, Supt.

Office

Vitriol Wks

Main Building

Office

Wharf

Ten't Hos
P.G. Co.

Ten't Hos
P.G. Co.

P.G. Co.
S.M. Norton

B.B. Smith
A. Healy
Rob't F. Doane
F.W. Shadley

B.C. Gifford
G.L. Gifford

S.M. Norton

Robt F. Doane

Mill

Liberty Hall

Market

Depot

Pummer
D.W.Bu

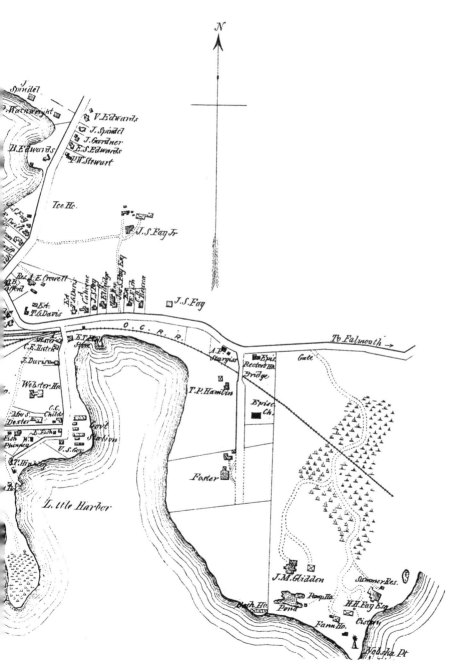

Ruth Anna's school was a private school taught by Miss Tappan in the basement of the Asa Shiverick house on the corner of Main and School Streets.

We commenced school* today. Miss Tappan brought our new books. We have two new German books, reader and grammar and a Rhetoric. She brought one history of England for us to read.

It snowed last night and spoilt the coasting but it may be worn down again. Isa came up street a little while this afternoon. Mr. Erasmus Gould of Falmouth died last night. Isa asked me to go tonight with her to the social aid so I went. Anna, Isie Spindel, Ellie, Isa Poor and myself were together. Had a very nice time indeed.

Drawing of Ruth Anna Hatch at school, from sketchbook of Eva March Tappan. Courtesy WHHC.

Its a very disagreeable day. It rains and the walking is awful. Did not come home to dinner but stayed at school. After school made cornballs. They were very good. Addie has been up to Cousin Abbie's two or three days.

Went to school as usual. In the afternoon, Grace, Isa and I went into the hatching house*

*at the Fish Commission quarters on Little Harbor, furnished by the Lighthouse Board

Buildings of the Lighthouse Board on Little Harbor where the Fish Commission obtained laboratory space for experiments in codfish hatching. Courtesy WHHC.

to see them hatch codfish. Some of them had already come out of the eggs. They are so small you can hardly see them. After that Grace and Isa came to my house and stayed to tea. We played words and they went home quite early. Nellie has been up to Abbie's spending the day.

SATURDAY, JANUARY 8, 1881

Very pleasant. I worked in the morning and put in a few stamps. Addie came home at noon. Isa came up in the afternoon for me to go to the fish commission again. First we went to the library. Mr. Poor went with us and this time we went up into the labratory and saw the fish under a microscope. You could see the heart beat just as plain as could be.

Papa came home tonight. Nellie and I gave Addie Longfellow poems Christmas but we did not like the book so got it exchanged and Papa brought it tonight.

SUNDAY, JANUARY 9, 1881

It is quite cold today but pleasant. Went to Church this morning to Sabbath School. I have been reading "Too Rich" today. Like it pretty well.

We heard that a little boy* who lives down in the factory neighborhood died of scarlet fever today. I hope it will not spread.

Spencer Baird, founder of the Fisheries laboratory in Woods Hole, and G.B. Goode seining in Little Harbor. Courtesy WHHC.

**John Glenn, 2 years and 4 months old*

Isa came for me to go to meeting with her. Dr. Rice preached again. Had a better sermon than I have heard him preach before. The wind blows quite hard. I guess the old "Range" which is leaking badly will get tipped over.

MONDAY, JANUARY 10, 1881

It is a horrid storm. Rained very hard in the morning and foggy in the afternoon. Cant hardly stand up it is so slippery. Papa went this morning and I went to the train with him. It rained so hard this noon Florence* made me stay to dinner. Had a letter from Myra today. She and Thankie each sent me a pretty card. Studied my lessons this evening but guess I shall have a sorry lesson tomorrow for I dont half know them.

* *Florence Davis*

Pacific Guano
Works on Long
Point, now
Penzance Point.
Between the years
1863 and 1889,
fertilizer was made
at "the factory"
from fish scraps and
guano. Courtesy
WHHC.

TUESDAY, JANUARY 11, 1881

It is pleasant but terrible slippery still. In the afternoon Miss Tappan and I went to walk over to the mowing hill. Had a good time though it was hard to stand up. In the evening

the society had their first monthly supper. It was held here. There were quite a lot who came, about 35 I should think. They all seemed to have a very nice time. Had supper about half past seven, and then we played games. Did not go home till after eleven. Isa went back home this morning. Guess I shall miss her.

Very pleasant. Went to school as usual. After school Miss Tappan and I went to walk. Went over to see the new Catholic Church which is just being built. We crossed the Eel pond to get there and then we went to the Mill Pond and got some pussy willows. Stopped into Ruth's a few minutes.

Hattie Shivericks father died yesterday very suddenly in Boston. Of heart disease I guess. Emma Davis is very sick. Cant use her feet and they are afraid of Congestion of brain.

The snow seems to be thawing today and there is not much left here. I have studied very hard all day and all this evening and my headaches. Guess we shall leave our Algebra this week. Will Cahoon was taken with the measles today and had to go home. Mr. Luscombe and Nellie, Brady Gifford and Bessie and Addie and Fred Gifford and some others went sleighing this evening. The snow is almost gone.

Interior of St. Joseph's Catholic Church on Millfield Street. Walls and ceiling were elaborately decorated by an Italian painter. Courtesy James McGrath.

They went to Waquoit and had supper at the Tobey House. Got home about one P.M. Had a nice time.

FRIDAY, JANUARY 14, 1881

Not very pleasant. Rained at night. Aunt Lucy is spending the day at our house. I stayed there to ten and we made candy in the evening. Aunt Lucy did not come home, it rained so hard and they made me stay all night there.

Played words and backgammon in the evening.

SATURDAY, JANUARY 15, 1881

A lovely day. After I got home from Josie's I went to Mr. Walsh's after milk and then put some stamps in my new book. Mr. Fay came in about dinner time and brought me a package of shells which he picked up in Florida. They were very pretty. In the afternoon Ellie came for me to go over to Nobsque skating but I could not get any girls to go with me. They said it was splendid skating. I was glad afterward that I did not go for Anna came over to see me. We went down to the Library and she stayed to tea.*

SUNDAY, JANUARY 16, 1881

Went to Church this morning. Its the loveliest day and quite cold. Hope there will be good skating tomorrow but am afraid it will storm. I have been reading "Pique" this afternoon.

I hear that Minnie Robinson is quite feeble. They are afraid she will have consumption. Emma Davis is better, I believe.

* Methodist

I went to meeting at the Chapel* tonight with Ruth Shiverick. There were quite a number there. Mr. Lovejoy preached. Wrote to Lizzie today and ought to have written many more letters.

MONDAY, JANUARY 17, 1881

Thought it was going to rain this morning but it cleared off pleasant in the afternoon. Miss Tappan, Josie, Ellie, Frank and Fred Gifford and myself went skating after school down on Nobsque Pond. It was lovely skating and had a very nice time. Went over to Anna's a minute and she came down on the pond to watch us. In the evening, Mother wanted me to down with her to Mrs. Joan Swifts so I went. Addie and Nellie went down to Bessie Shivericks this afternoon and stayed to tea.

Methodist Church built in 1879 on Water Street. In 1948 it was moved to a site on School Street and Maury Lane and is now called Endeavor House. Courtesy WHHC.

TUESDAY, JANUARY 18, 1881

A cold day but very lovely. Went to school as usual. After school went down to the Eel Pond skating. It was not so good as the Nobsque Pond was but I had a nice time.

All the schools were there and Ellie, Ben Gifford and the two other Giffords. Herbert Childs I believe has the chicken pox. I did not go to the society which was at his house for Mother was not sure I had had it. The girls went and had a nice time. It is Ellie's birthday today. He is sixteen.

It snowed a few minutes this morning, just enough to cover the ice. However after school we all went down to Nobsque skating. The Shiverick girls, Addie and Nellie, Miss Tappan, Josie, Fred, Ellie and I went. The snow did not hurt it much and we stayed till dark and had a lovely time.

We are having the piazza torn away and a new one put up so can't go out the front door. In the evening I made caramels and studied.

It is a lovely day. After school Miss Tappan and I went to walk over to Bay Shore. It was very pleasant. There was a dance at the hall in the evening. We all went after Bible Class which was at our house. I did not expect to go till about four o'clock. Charrie Purdum had five of her New Bedford friends come over on purpose to go. Guess they had a nice time. There were more than forty there. I danced all the time and with Isa Spindel most of the time. Cousin Jotham took me down to get Oyster Stew. All had a very nice time.

Ice skating on Nobska Pond, ca. 1900. Fay water tower and ice house in background to left, Nobska Lighthouse in background to right. Courtesy WHHC.

A perfectly horrible easterly storm. Addie and Nettie Shiverick went to New Bedford this morning to come back tomorrow. They have got an awful day.

Did not come home to dinner today it stormed so hard. Nellie and Frank put cards in her new album. Lizzie went to Lynn day before yesterday with her father. They have got the floor laid to the new piazza.

Got up late. After I worked a little while I put some more stamps in my new-book. It seems as if I never should get them all changed.

In the afternoon I went to the library and after that skated on the Eel Pond until after six o'clock.

Papa and Addie came in the train. Papa brought me sixty stamps that I did not have. Some were quite rare. I have about 560 in all, now.

A nice day. Went to Church this morning but as usual I stayed at home and read in the afternoon. "Old Mam'selle's Secret" was the name of the book I read. Think it is splendid. I ought to have written at least two letters but did not write one.

Ruth and I went to meeting at the hall tonight. Mr. Rice's sermon was about who wrote the Bible.

I like him better than I used to. Mr. Carleton* called in this evening.

* Rector of the Church of the Messiah, 1867-1881

MONDAY, JANUARY 24, 1881

Very pleasant and lovely skating on Nobsque Pond. Went there after school with Frank, Fred, Josie, Miss Tappan and Ellie.

Nero* and Nep went with us and got to fighting when they got there. I could not send Nero home so had to go way back with him. When I got back to the pond I was rather tired. However, I skated till almost dark. My going home did not do much good for after I had been skating awhile Nero came back and had to stay all the rest of the time.

* Ruth Anna's dog

Papa went back this morning.

TUESDAY, JANUARY 25, 1881

It is still good skating but did not go today. The society was up to Florence's but I had my lessons to learn and when I got through it was so late I would not go.

Nothing special took place today that I know of.

Original wooden Church of the Messiah at right, consecrated in 1854 and still used for church purposes. Rectory at left built in 1877. Courtesy WHHC.

After school I went skating a little while but went up to Mrs. Carleton's and called first. It was pretty windy on the pond and quite cold. Most froze before I got home.

Addie and Mother went up to Florence's to spend the evening. I don't go much of anywhere evenings on account of studying.

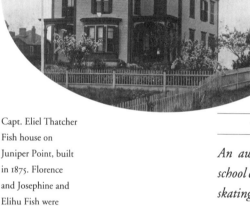

Capt. Eliel Thatcher Fish house on Juniper Point, built in 1875. Florence and Josephine and Elihu Fish were friends of Ruth Anna and her family. On the extreme left is the Butler house. Courtesy WHHC.

THURSDAY, JANUARY 27, 1881

An awful windy day and very cold. After school came right home. It was too windy to go skating. The piazza is almost done. Like the rail very much. Nellie & Frank worked on her scrap book. They went to the Bible Class in the evening. Addie & I stayed at home. I had a letter from Cousin Sarah Roland today. She (sent) me some Confederate Stamps and a sheet of Confederate ten dollar bills.

Heard today that Mr. Look and his wife had separated. Minnie Robinson does not seem to get any better.

FRIDAY, JANUARY 28, 1881

After school I went down to Ruth Shivericks and Katie Donaldson and Persis came in while I was there. They made us all stay to*

Persis Crowell

new books. We have [
new German books, ready
grammar, and a Rhe[
She brought me a histor[
England forms to rea[

It snowed last ni[
and spoilt the coa[
but it may [snow] down
again. Tea came [
but a little while [
afternoon. Mr. Chaenn[
Gould of Falmouth die[
night. Tea asked me
to night with her to th[
aide so I went. Anna,
[ ]ndel, & Elie, Tea [ ]oa [

Ruth Anna Hatch's
house at far right
with its new piazza,
in the northwest
corner of Little
Harbor. A Woods
Hole spritsail boat
ready for a sail is
tied up at dock in
front of the Hatch
house. Photo by
Baldwin Coolidge,
1895. Courtesy
WHHC.

supper. Persis was going to stay all night and after Katie went home they tried to make me stay to, so after a while I had to say I would. Had a very nice time.

It is an awful windy day.

Crowell House, built in 1871. Horse and wagon on School Street, just beyond Shiverick's back yard. Courtesy WHHC.

SATURDAY, JANUARY 29, 1881

*After I got home this morning which was about nine I put in about sixty stamps in my book. After dinner, I changed my clothes and went down to the Library.** *

*It was very good skating on the Mill Pond but it was too windy to skate. Mrs. Crowell had another daughter born today.** Quite a family.*

This afternoon I read a bad boys diary which Persis let me take. It is very funny. Papa did not come home tonight. Miss Tappan, Josie and I took a short walk this P.M.

* The Library was set up in a small room at the southwest corner of the basement in Liberty Hall.

*Mertie Crowell

A snow storm but not very hard. Sunday passed off as it always does.

Church in the morning; read Princess of Thule in the afternoon but did not go to meeting in the evening as it was not very pleasant. Wrote a long letter to Isa today and ought to have written other letters.

Frank came home in the evening as usual and we had "popcorn and milk".

Nothing special happened today. The girls spent the afternoon at Florence's.

Miss Tappan and I took a short walk down in the Valley and over School Street. Studied in the evening.

Papa went to Lynn yesterday and spent Sunday. Said he had a nice time.

Woods Hole railroad depot and yard showing turntable and roundhouse. Photo by Baldwin Coolidge, 1896. Courtesy WHHC.

The society was at Char
Purdums this evening.
I went and had a
very nice time. Played
Casino and listened
to the music.

John Carleton came
home for a short vacation
tonight. He was a beauty
I believe.

Nellie staid to tea
here and went to the
society with us in the
evening.

WEDNESDAY, FEBRUARY 2, 1881

A nice day. Florence.
Miss Tappan, Josie and
Ellie came here to tea
this afternoon. I went to
the library with Bessie
this afternoon to take
Florence's place but she
did not need me to help.
They had a nice time
here I guess. We played
games in the evening.
It is very cold weather.
The coldest I have known
almost since I can re-
member. The harbor is
frozen hard and people
have walked from Mr. Fay's
to Mr. Foster's wharf.

The society was at Charrie Purdums this evening. I went and had a very nice time. Played Casino and listened to the music.

John Carleton came home for a short vacation tonight. He wears a beaver I believe.

Nettie staid to tea here and went to the society with us in the evening.

A nice day. Florence, Miss Tappan, Josie and Ellie came here to tea this afternoon. I went to the library with Bessie this afternoon to take Florence's place but she did not need me to help.

The *Range* in Little Harbor with the Church of the Messiah in background. From the sketchbook of Eva March Tappan. Courtesy WHHC.

They had a nice time here I guess. We played games in the evening.

It is very cold weather. The coldest I have known almost since I can remember. The harbor is frozen hard and people have walked from Mr. Fay's to Mr. Foster's wharf.

After school Miss Tappan, Ellie and I went to walk down to Butler's Point. It was lovely there. We went out quite a little way on the ice. After we came from there we walked out on Little Harbor to the Range and climbed all over. It seemed very funny to be walking in the harbor. The girls went to Bible Class in the evening.

After school, Frank took me to ride a little way in his Uncle Benjamin's carriage. He is gone away and Frank uses the horse and carriage. After I came home, tried to make vinegar candy in a paper basket. Had quite good luck.

In the evening I went down to Ruth Shivericks a little while, while the girls were at the sing in John Swift's. We played words and I had a very nice time.

After I came home from riding in the afternoon I went into the auction room in the basement of the Chapel.* Bought two combs.

* *The basement of the Methodist Church was rented as a store and the proceeds went to help pay expenses.*

Got up abut nine o'clock this morning. Put in a few stamps in my book. Ruth Shiverick came in a little while about noon. In the afternoon, Frank carried me down to Nobsque Pond in the carriage and I skated till most dark.

The Nantucket school teacher was there skating. He is a perfect skater. There were lots of people there. After I came home I went down to the train to meet Papa and then Addie, Nettie, Bessie and I went into the Auction. Had a nice time but was tired standing up.

Stamps courtesy
Falmouth Stamp
and Coin.

Butler (now Juniper)
Point with paddle
wheel steamer
heading out to the
Vineyard. Photo by
Baldwin Coolidge.
Courtesy WHHC.

Quite pleasant but the ground and ice are thawing. It is very bad walking. Went to Church both morning and afternoon and to the hall in the evening.

Mr. Messer is going South on the schooner "Harry Messer" Tuesday and Mrs. Messer is going West the same day. He talks of taking Nero with him for company. I shall feel awfully if he does and I have been feeling badly all evening.

Possibly Ruth Anna Hatch skating on Nobska Pond with her friends. Photo by Sarah Bryant Fay, 1881. Courtesy WHHC.

Very pleasant indeed. After school Mr. Messer invited us to go down to the "Harry Messer" and see her. Florence, Josie, Ellie, Miss Tappan, Nellie, Addie, Bessie, Nettie and Celine Smith and Mr. Messer all went in one work wagon. The Vessel was splendid. I would like to go there and I don't blame Nero for wanting to go South but I don't think he will go.

The cabin was splendid and the vessel is a large one, We had fun there but it smelt badly.

In evening I worked worsted work. Papa went today.

A perfectly beautiful day. After school, Frank took Nellie, Beck Davis and I down to Falmouth. We had the best carriage. It was lovely riding though terribly muddy. John Carleton came in and worked on Addie's crazy cushion. He stayed to tea and we trained awfully. They went to Bible class in the evening. Mrs. Messer started today but there was not wind enough for the ship to go. Nero is not going.

Heard that Hattie Shiverick's grandmother was dead. It is the third death in that family within four months.

After school, Miss Tappan and I went to walk over to the orchard and picked some apple tree buds to see if they would not flower quicker in the house. Then we went down to the ice pond and got some pussy willows. They were almost all bloomed out.

In the evening we all went to the auction. Mother got some dishes and some paper for me to take to school. It is the worst walking I think I ever saw in Wood's Holl.

The "Harry Messer" did not go today. No wind.

A horrid sort of day. The sun has not been out and the walking is still wretched. Mr. Messer took Bob's kitten, Midge, off in the "Harry

Quissett 11 March 1881

The undersigned agree to pay the sum set against our respective names for the purpose of building a Hall in this village

Names	Amount
a. Ward m. Parker	X 50
a. E. N. Ryder	X 5
Lorenzo Eldred	X 10
W. H. Sweet	X 10
C. N. Davis	X 10
John Rogers	X 50
James H. Davis	X 5
Francis Davis	X 5
~~Ira H. Davis~~	X
Mrs Hannah Davis	X 5
F. P. Davis	X 10
Wm. C. Davis	X 5
Mary D. Davis	X 5
Mary A. Lawrence	X 5
R. C Bodfish	Pd X 5
Geo E Clarke	X 10
J. Davis	X 2
J. H. Davis	X 5
E. L. Fish	X 16 5
Mr & Mrs Carr	X 25

Messer" instead of the dog. She was awful cunning and I was sorry to have her go. But she had better go than the dog.

Hear they are going to build a hall down to Quissette. The great supper talked about so long came off tonight. The three societies joined. We had bake beans, indian pudding, cake, etc. After supper played rope and blind man's bluff. I did not play rope. Will Cahoon came home with me because he could not get A.

FRIDAY, FEBRUARY 11, 1881

My sixteenth birthday! I feel very old indeed. that is, I don't feel any older but it seems old to think of it.

It was foggy in the morning; cleared off lovely in the afternoon. Papa and Mother gave me a wide gold ring with my initials on the outside and the date inside.

The girls gave me the set of arms flags and rulers for my stamp book. They are very pretty. Miss Tappan painted me a locket and grandma gave me a dollar. Ruth gave me a knife and Miss Lewers a card and Cousin Charles some ribbon.

Yesterday afternoon Miss Tappan and I went to walk down in the woods and after that I went down to Ruth Shiverick's and stayed to tea. At noon I had a card from Boston but dont know who sent it.

Birthday cards of the period. Courtesy Bertha Hill.

SATURDAY, FEBRUARY 12, 1881

A horrid dismal day. Put in stamps and some of the rulers in my book. Grandma went home this morning before it rained and Nellie went with her to help her a few days. Had a letter from Lizzie day before yesterday and she sent me her picture.

SUNDAY, FEBRUARY 13, 1881

Very windy but pleasant. Went to Church in the morning. In the afternon all but I went to Church. I stayed at home and read "Miles Standish" out loud. At supper I went to reach over for the cream and tipped it over it went all over the table, floor and my green and blue dress. I thought my dress was spoilt, the cream was so rich, but it does not show yet.

In the evening went to the hall to meeting.

Did not feel well but went to school. Did not have a Valentine for the whole day! Just think of it! After school Miss Tappan, Nero and I went to walk a little way. After I came home, made a little molasses candy. Quite good.

Read some but not far in "Mosees from an old Manse". Like it very much. Went to bed early. Nellie stays up to Grandma's.

Tim Hamblin had a daughter born today.

After school, Josie, Ellie, Miss Tappan, the two dogs and I went to walk. We walked a long way. Down to this side of Quissette Harbor and took a long way home. Got very tired.

The society was at Ruth Shiverick's. She came up and teazed me to go or I should not have gone. Had a nice time though there were not many there. I hear that Mr. Foster Hatch is going to move to New Bedford to take charge work in a new factory there.

Valentines of the period. Courtesy Bertha Hill.

Stormed hard all the morning but cleared off in the afternoon.

Ellie took his first music lesson this afternoon of John Swift. I want to take of him very much. I try to keep in practise but don't very well.

This evening I went to the auction with the girls. There were lots there. I bought a pair of scissors for five cents. They will do to cut paper.

Saw Gracie there and she says Anna Hubbard's
father is going to leave. I am awful sorry.

A lovely day. After school went to walk down
to Quissette. We saw the new hall which they
have begun.

Stopped in to Grandmas on the way home and
played on the organ a little.

We have been having new banisters in the
entry. They are not done yet but they look nice
so far. Nellie's room is being papered and
painted. The new piazza is a great improve-
ment to the house. Bible Class here tonight.

After school I went down to Ruth Shiverick's
awhile. Lottie Edwards had a party in the
evening. A surprise party. Ellie and Isie were
invited but I was not. They said I was too old
but guess the trouble was they wanted more
boys. I went up to Grandma's and spent the
evening and stayed all night with her.

Mr. Butler is here and Uncle Tim does not get
home till late. Anna came in a little while
before meeting. I had a very pretty valentine
from Cousin Charles, I think.

Stayed and helped Grandma till ten o'clock
and after. Then I came home. After dinner

The Asa Shiverick
house on the corner
of Main and School
Streets where Miss
Tappan's private
school was held.
The building was
moved in 1949 to
School Street,
between the Meth-
odist Church and
Crowell House.
Courtesy WHHC.

went over to Gracie's but she was not at home. Went down to the library and afterwards to Mrs. Poor's a little while.

Papa came home in the train. He went down to Auction and bought a basket of apples, a yellow dish and some paper. This pencil is horrible. I had a little valentine. Don't know who sent it.

A lovely day. Went down to Church in the morning and spent the afternoon as I usually do - reading and writing letters. Went to meeting in the evening at the hall. I have got to carry in a composition tomorrow. That is, I ought to and guess I shan't. Wrote to Cousin Sarah Holland.

A snow storm. After school did not do much of anything. Papa and Mother are papering Nellie's room. It is painted olive shades and papered with the same colors. It looks pretty I think.

Wrote my composition this evening.

Washing's (sic) birthday. We only had school about an hour and a half in morning. After that I went up to Mr. Butler's. He and some friends are here and Julia. I heard Harry was sick with diphteria and went to see how he was. He is better but has been quite sick, I guess.

In the afternoon went down to Ruth Shiverick's a little while but did not find her home. Went to Gracie's first and stayed quite a while.

Papa went this morning. Did not have school this afternoon because we finished our lessons this morning. I stayed home all the afternoon. Nellie and Addie went to Grandma's to spend the day so mother and I were alone. Miss Tappan and Josie came in a little while in the evening.

A very cold day. The (weather) has changed suddenly.

Grace was to have gone over to Anna's with me today but she did not come. So I went down to Ruth's a few minutes. Did not stay long.

Studied all evening while the girls were at Bible Class.

A hard snow but it is very light so guess it won't last long. Did not come home right (after) school but stayed and learnt my Monday's lessons. Then Josie would not let me go home so I stayed to supper. Ellie and I acted awfully. We made candy after supper and Sadie came up. We played Old Maid, Everlasting and Muggins.

Went up to Grandma's about ten o'clock and stayed to dinner. Did not get up till nearly nine.

Cousin Abbie came tonight. She has been to Lynn making a visit. Miss Tappan and I went to walk this afternoon.

Went to Church this morning. Spent the rest of the day in eating and trying to find something to do. Frank stayed to dinner here.

Went to meeting in the evening and it was about the worst walking I ever saw. It was very foggy, not a star out and mud up to your ankles. Lost my rubber off once.

A very dismal day and everybody feels badly.

Went up to Grandma's a little while after school. It rained hard about noon and I stayed to dinner at school.

Had a letter from Lizzie and she is coming here next week which is her vacation. The first class is going to graduate at Fairhaven this week. Lizzie Babcock and Carrie Sampson are in it.

Wish I was there to see them.

Not very pleasant.
Addie does not feel
well. She has a headach
Miss Tappan and I
went to walk this after
noon. We went over to
Bay Shore and got some
pussy willows back of
Emma Edwards.
My apple blossoms
that I picked some
time ago are coming out
nicely. hope they will
bloom. Went to the
society this evening. It
was at Mrs. Dexter's. Mr.
Carter the school teacher was
there. I think he is very queer
Mc Cahoon came home agai
because Addie was not there

March

Josie, Miss Tappan and I
went to walk a little way
over to Mr. Glidden's. It
was bad walking.
Josie and Miss T. came in
and stayed to tea. We
played cards in the eve-
ning and I did not learn
my German lesson till
they went home.

Not very pleasant. Addie does not feel well. She has a headache. Miss Tappan and I went to walk this afternoon. We went over to Bay Shore and got some pussy willows back of Emma Edward's. My apple blossoms that I picked some time ago are coming out nicely; hope they will bloom. Went to the society this evening. It was at Mrs. Dexter's. Mr. Carter, the school teacher was there. I think he is very queer. Will Cahoon came home again because Addie was not there.

Members of the Glidden family at the water tower for their house overlooking Nobska Pond, ca. 1881. John M. Glidden was treasurer of the Pacific Guano Company and owned a large estate on Nobska Point. Courtesy Boynton Glidden.

WEDNESDAY, MARCH 2, 1881

Josie, Miss Tappan and I went to walk a little way over to Mr. Glidden's. It was bad walking.

Josie and Miss T. came in and stayed to tea. We played cards in the evening and I did not learn my German lesson till they went home.

THURSDAY, MARCH 3, 1881

Still raining and has been all the week. Addie is down with a toothache and Mother isn't very well. Ellie did not come to school today for (he) is sick. Sadie staid to tea here this afternoon and went down to Ruth Shiverick's a minute after supper. Lizzie Healey was there.

Lizzie Sanford is coming over next week to stay awhile.

Raining for a change. Mother feels quite badly and Addie's toothache is no better and Ellie is still sick. Heard that Minnie Robinson was worse. They had a doctress from Boston and she did not give them much encouragement.

Suppose it is President Garfield and ex-President Hayes by this time. They had a nice day. Rains like everything. I had a paper and Addie had a little book from Mr. Messer who is in Florida. It came this noon.

Pleasant at last. It has been a whole week that we have had nothing but rain and fog and it seems lovely to have pleasant weather again. Went up to Grandma's and helped her this morning. This afternoon went over to Gracie's to see if she would go to Anna's with me. She couldn't because she had to tie tags. So I went alone; that is with Nero. I did not mean to stay long but they made me stay to tea. Had a real nice time and Anna came almost home with me. Papa came tonight and brought Addie's writing desk for her birthday.*

Pussy willows, from
the sketchbook of
Eva March Tappan.
Courtesy WHHC.

*For the West
Falmouth Tag Factory

It is sort of a gray day. Went to Church this morning as usual. Mr. Carleton changed the afternoon service to seven o'clock in the evening. Went and liked it very much. Quite a lot of people there.

Birthday cards of
the period. Courtesy
Bertha Hill.

MONDAY, MARCH 7, 1881

Addie's birthday. Besides her writing desk, she had a pair of silver pins from Cousin Charles, Cards from most all the girls, a vase from Minnie Robinson. Minnie is not well at all.

TUESDAY, MARCH 8, 1881

The society was at Sadie's. There were very few there. We played cards and that's all. Had quite a good time.

Ellie is quite sick. The doctor says he has inflammatory rheumatism and his chest is filling with water.

WEDNESDAY, MARCH 9, 1881

Nothing special happened. Ellie is not any better. Addie's toothache is well. Frank is going away next week. Guess we will miss him.

Addie had a lovely card from Mr. Hill today. It was meant for her birthday but was a little late. He painted it himself on a white wood panel. The picture was pansies. Just as natural as could be.

THURSDAY, MARCH 10, 1881

Last night they sent for the doctor for Ellie is worse; he did not come but he sent some medicine. I guess he is quite sick. He is about the same today.

Expected Lizzie tonight and I went to the train at the usual time. While I was waiting a telegram came saying the train had run off the track at Brockton and would not be here till nine o'clock. So I went home and came down to the train again at nine and Lizzie did not come after all. I was provoked. Don't know why she didn't come.

Ellie is a little better, I believe.

SATURDAY, MARCH 12, 1881

I raced all over the place on errands today and am just as tired as I can be.

Thought Lizzie would come in the noon train as much as could be but she didn't come. Had a card saying she was not very well and would not come till Monday. About train time at night I was sitting down and who should come in but Aunt Sarah and Lizzie. We did not expect Aunt Sarah and had given up expecting Lizzie.

SUNDAY, MARCH 13, 1881

Pleasant in the morning and evening both. Stayed to Grandma's to lunch. Ellie is getting better.

MONDAY, MARCH 14, 1881

Lizzie went to school with me this morning. Didn't do much of anything the rest of the day. Frank went this morning. Don't know (where) he is going.

Went in to see Ellie a few minutes this morning. He looks just as pale and thin as can be.

Addie was invited by Will Cahoon to go to Falmouth and hear the concert by the Choral union. Nearly all the girls and boys went.

Uncle Tim took Lizzie and I down to Falmouth to ride this afternoon. It was lovely riding. We went into Mrs. Clarke's and called . Went to the society at Mrs. Carleton's.

After school Lizzie and I went to the library and then to walk. We had a splendid walk over to Mr. Glidden's and then down on the beach. The waves were lovely - real high. We sat down quite a while and then came home. Didn't do much in the evening.

Mr. Butler's, now Crane, house built in 1880 on Butler's Point. Courtesy WHHC.

Ellie wasn't so well yesterday and they sent for the doctor but he is better today and guess he will get along.

THURSDAY, MARCH 17, 1881

Didn't do anything all day but in the evening Ruth Shiverick came up and spent the evening. Played words. She invited us down to spend the afternoon Saturday if Lizzie does not go home then. Don't think she will go till Monday.

Mother, Aunt Sarah and Abbie went to Boston this morning to come home tomorrow night. She is going to get me a dress.

FRIDAY, MARCH 18, 1881

We walked all over Mr. Butler's place this afternoon. Had a very nice time. Mother came home tonight. My dress is an olive green check. I think I shall like it. Cousin Abbie gave me a darling little glove buttoner with a fan on it.

SATURDAY, MARCH 19, 1881

We went up to Grandmothers and stayed to dinner. Aunt Sarah thought they had better go today as it was pleasant so they went. It rained hard though at night. Went up to see Ellie and Miss Tappan after the train went. Ellie is drest - Miss Tappan is coming here to stay Monday.

Papa came tonight. Frank is at Attleboro but don't know how long he will stay there.

Went to Church morning and evening. Nothing particular to write. Miss Tappan is coming tomorrow. The school room is fixed all it is going to be. Guess it will do. Miss Lizz.

Miss Tappan came this morning and we had school though Cousin Eliel did not bring by desk and the rest of the books till nearly noon.

Ellie won't come back to school till after vacation which begins a week from Wednesday. I may go to Boston to stay a night and then go right to Fairhaven. If I go I shall go the same day Miss Tappan does - Wednesday. Society was this evening because there is a time at Quissette tomorrow night. It was at Abbie's.

A lovely day. After dinner Miss Tappan and I went to Nobsque to walk. She drew Nobsque light and while she was drawing, I read.

Then we took a walk through the woods home. The Quissette was dedicated tonight. Addie was invited by Fred. I wanted to go awfully

March 18, '81.

Wooded pool,
March 18, 1881.
From the sketch-
book of Eva
March Tappan.
Courtesy WHHC.

Nobska Lighthouse, built in 1876 to replace the original light built on top of the keeper's house in 1829. Courtesy WHHC.

*Spencer Fullerton Baird, who chose Woods Hole as the site for the Fish Commission Station.

but of course could not. They had a very nice time and a supper of chicken pie, coffee, ice cream, etc.

WEDNESDAY, MARCH 23, 1881

Rather glad after all that I did not go to Quissette. Everybody that went is sick with a sort of cholera morbus. Addie is sick, too, though no one is very sick. They can't imagine what the matter is. Even the boys are sick. All the Quisette and Falmouth folks, too. Guess it is something about the chicken pie.

Everybody is wondering what the reason is. I have not done anything special today.

THURSDAY, MARCH 24, 1881

Ellie spent the day with us today. He is getting better fast, I think.

Cousin Charles came in this morning and said the mystery about the Quissettee affair is partially solved. Prof. Baird,* when he was here had a chicken pie made. When he saw it, he would not eat because he said a chicken pie without a hole in the top was poisonous. He said the air could not escape if there was no hole in it. That is the only reason they can find.

FRIDAY, MARCH 25, 1881

Grace and I were going to visit school this afternoon but we found that no one else was going so we went over to Anna's instead. We stayed awhile and then I brought Anna home with me to stay all night, because there was to *be an entertainment at the hall. We went and it was not very good. A man whistled the Mocking Bird and Home Sweet Home lovely. That was about the only good thing in the entertainment.*

SATURDAY, MARCH 26, 1881

Anna had to go home early so I got up and walked as far as the Church with her. It was only a little past six. It seems very funny to be up early. I spent about three hours mending my dress today. Thought I must be doing something towards getting ready to go to Boston.

Went down to the library this afternoon. Last time I got "Jack and Jill". Think it is lovely. Papa did not come home tonight. Ruth and Persis went to Boston this morning.

SUNDAY, MARCH 27, 1881

Went to Church morning and evening. Intended to go to the hall to the sabbath school concert but could not get anyone to go with me. It was to be a grand concert.

Wrote to Lizzie. It seems as if I cannot wait for school to be out so I can go to Boston. I shant stay more than one night though.

MONDAY, MARCH 28, 1881

Very windy. Have not done anything special. Josie invited Nellie and Miss Tappan and I to go to Falmouth with her to get the horse shod this afternoon. We went, and had a good time.

49

Ruth Anna Hatch?
March 25, 1881.
From the sketch-
book of Eva
March Tappan.
Courtesy WHHC.

*While we were waiting walked over Mr.
Beebe's place and got frightened at an awful
bull dog and had fun. Miss Tappan stayed at
Josie's to tea.*

---

*Looks as though it would storm tomorrow.
Finished school for this term and I guess I am
glad.*

*This afternoon, I picked up the things I am to
carry, washed, ironed and starched some lace
and a collar, and then Miss Tappan and I took
a walk. Went to the society at Mrs. Swift's.
Intended to come home early but got interested
and stayed till after ten.*

---

*It stormed in the first place but not very hard
when we started. Got rather tired riding such
a long way. When we got there it began to rain
quite hard.*

*Miss Tappan and I went around to Jordan
Marsh's and Houghton Ward and Gay's and
lots of other places and then we got dinner. She
left me about two, and I found my way down
to the store where I stayed till nearly six and
then went to Abbie's. She took me to her room.
In the evening Papa, Abbie and I went to hear
"Olivette" at the Gaity in an awful snow storm
but the opera was just splendid.*

Stormy still. After breakfast I went and got me a pair of gloves, yellowish ones. Then went to the store where Mr. Morrison was to meet me and take me to the State House and Art Museum. I waited till nearly twelve and he did not come so went to Abbie's. In the afternoon found my way up to Hancock St., where Mrs. Holbrook lives. Had a nice call there and then she went around down street with me. Papa got me a pair of glasses, really nice ones. In the evening he came up to Abbie's a while. It stormed hard all day.

Stormy still. After breakfast I went and got me
a pair of gloves, yellow rich
ones. Then went to the
store where Mrs. Morison was
to meet me and take me
to the State House and
Art Museum. I waited
till nearly twelve and
he did not come so went
crabbie. In the afternoon
found my way up to
Dancroft St. where Mrs.
Holbrook lives. Had a nice
call there and then she
went round down street
with me. Papa got me a
pair of glasses, real nice ones
In the evening he came
up to the house a while

April

A lovely day at last. It
seems too good to be true.
Papa went up to the Art
Museum with me at ten
and we stayed till one.
It was lovely there. We got
dinner at Barnede and then
went to the State House
and in to the Senate
Gallery and heard the sena-
tor speak. Then I went to
Dan Marshes and then to
the store where I waited till
time to go to Abbie's. In the
evening Papa came up and
asked us to go somewhere.
Abbie was too tired to go but Papa
and I decided to go to the
gas Minstrels at the Globe. The
Theatre was crowded and the

There was a very nice Remarklass I expected.

FRIDAY, APRIL 1, 1881

A lovely day at last. It seems too good to be true. Papa went up to the Art Museum with me at ten and we stayed till one. It was lovely there. We got dinner at Barned's and then went to the State House and in to Senate Gallery and heard the Senators speak. Then I went to Jordan Marsh's and then to the store where I waited till time to go to Abbie's. In the evening Papa came up and wanted us to go somewhere. Abbie was too tired to go but Papa and I decided to go to the Negro Minstrels at the Globe. The Theatre was crowded and the play was very nice. Better than I expected.

SATURDAY, APRIL 2, 1881

Another lovely day and my last one in Boston. After breakfast Abbie helped me carry my bundles down to the store where I stayed till dinner time and then went to Abbie's. After dinner I went to Abbie's store and got me a hat. It is a turban, blue and white trimmed with wide blue plaid ribbon. It cost only two dollars at wholesale price. Papa and I left Boston at four; he for Wood's Holl and I for Fairhaven. He left me at Tremont where I met Uncle Tim. Got to Fairhaven at half past six. For the evening went over to Aunt Maria's.

SUNDAY, APRIL 3, 1881

Rather windy today. Went to Sabbath School in the morning and Church or meeting in the afternoon with Lizzie. Wrote to Nellie and

Papa. Lizzie's Aunt Lucy, Sarah Maria and the baby are visiting at Aunt Maria's and they came here to dinner. Aunt Maria, Uncle George, Mattie and Edith came, too. In the evening Lizzie and I went to meeting at the brick Church.

Called on Mrs. Nye during the day. Had a letter (from) Mother last night.

MONDAY, APRIL 4, 1881

Pleasant. Went over to New Bedford at a little before eleven to make an appointment with Dr. McLeod about my teeth. Have got to go Wednesday noon. Mother wrote me that Florence and Josie were coming over today so I started to look for them and met Florence on the street. Josie was having her teeth filled. I went to dinner with them and we shopped some and then I came back about half three. We stayed at home in the evening. Sarah Maria, Aunt Lucy and Warren came here today to stay.

TUESDAY, APRIL 5, 1881

Pleasant. Went to school with Lizzie this morning. Had a nice time. Her teacher is very sick and Miss Fairchild takes charge of it. Mr. Tripp is cutting his wisdom teeth and they are afraid he will have lockjaw. Lizzie stayed out of school this afternoon so that Sarah Maria could show her how to do a mat. We all helped. In the evening Aunt Sarah and Lucy, Matt, Lizzie and Maria and I went over to New Bedford to Liberty Hall. Its a theatre and the play was the "Cricket on the Hearth". It was very good.

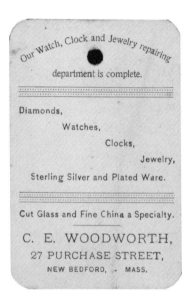

Shopping list for
New Bedford store.
Courtesy WHHC.

Lizzie went to school and at eleven I went to the dentist's and had a tooth filled. It almost killed me. In the afternoon the Brockton folks went home. Nellie Jackson came up and spent the evening with Lizzie and I. We had a good deal of fun and Nellie went home around nine. I think she is real nice.

Today is fast day so Lizzie wont have to go to school and there is not to be any school tomorrow. I went to Dr. McLeod's at twelve and had another tooth filled and have got to go once more. Tried to do a few errands in New Bedford but the stores were closed. This afternoon Lizzie and I worked on a mat a little while. We went down to the sociable in the vestry at six and got supper there. We had quite a nice time. Had a letter from Mother tonight.

Lizzie and I went to New Bedford at half past eleven. The doctor told me to come at quarter of twelve but he had such a rush he could not attend to me till after one. We got lunch at the Holly Tree lunch.

We got home about three. We were invited over to Mattie's to tea but we called on Lizzie Babcock first. She has an awful cold. then we went to Mattie's and found she had invited Nellie Jackson there to surprise us. We had a nice time.

A perfect day. Not a breath of wind and not a cloud. Aunt Sarah gave me one of the mats she was making. I hadn't the least idea it was for me. Then she gave me a real pretty birch bark picture. I packed my things in the morning and went down street with Lizzie. About twelve we started for New Bedford as we had some errands to do. I bought a Japanese frame for Addie to put her cards in. The boat left about half past one. Met Lulie Davis so had company over.

I was quite glad to get home.

I did not go to Church today because I was so tired but I went this evening. John Carleton is at home spending his vacation. He had a friend with him.

All the folks liked my hat that I got. I may wear it next Sunday which is Easter. Papa did not come home last night.

This is the last day of our vacation. Nellie and I went May flowering in the afternoon and we got some very pretty ones though it is quite early as yet, for them. I carried mine into Minnie Robinson's. She liked them very much.

I went to the train to meet Miss Tappan. I don't want to go to school a bit.

Ellie came to school today for the first day since he has been sick. We are going to study Roman History and we have a new German dictionary and "William Tell". It is a rainy day. Ellie staid to dinner though not because it rained. Miss Tappan and I went to walk after Mayflowers in all the storm. We got a few and got very wet besides. Went down to Ruth Shiverick's a while. She has a new teacher. A Mr. Heyward. They like him.

Another rainy day. Went down to the library in the afternoon and read "Louisiana" in the evening. Not a very brilliant day.

Spring blossoms. From the sketch-book of Eva March Tappan. Courtesy WHHC.

Abbie came here in the afternoon to cut my new spring dress. After school Nellie and Miss Tappan and I went Mayflowering. We got quite pretty ones but I don't think they are going to be very plenty this year. When I got home found Ruth Shiverick here who had come for me to stay all night. Her Aunt Betsey is dead and everyone is at Dennis but Bessie and Ruth. I had my lesson to learn so Ruth staid at my house to supper and then I went home with her.

I had to come home quite early on account of school. It is Good Friday today and we were going to have school out early so we could go to Church but it rained hard and there was no service. Ruth Shiverick came up again this evening for me to stay all night with her so I went.

Addie staid last night and tonight with Bessie.

SATURDAY, APRIL 16, 1881

Went up to Grandma's after I got home from Ruth's. I swept and cleaned up the front chamber and Uncle Tim's room and the kitchen. After dinner Nellie, Miss T. and I scoured the woods for mayflowers and did not find many after all. In the evening we went all round the place to carry our easter cards and we had some ourselves. I had one from Cousin Charlie and it was a beauty (with fringe round it). I also had one from Nellie, Frank and Josie. They were all pretty.

Ruth Anna Hatch's grandparents' house on School Street, at the left center of the photograph, is the second oldest house in Woods Hole. Courtesy WHHC.

Went to Church of course. The Church looked very pretty. Mrs. Foster had sent a super Altar and very pretty pair of candle sticks and they were used for the first time today.

Miss Turner sent a lovely crown and then we had lovely flowers from around here. On the organ was a pillow of pansies and there was a large stand of flowers where the font stands. On one side of chancel was a calla lily with three flowers on it and on the other side were some Easter lilies.

Pleasant. After school, Josie, Miss Tappan, Nero and I went to walk over to Bay Shores. We had a lovely walk and lay on the shore throwing stones to the dog. It seemed just like summer. Coming home we saw Captain Gibbs' catrigged boat just coming into the harbor. He is going to let Ellie use it until he gets ready to sell it.

I had a letter from Isa Poor this noon. It is the first letter I have had since she went back at New York.

After school, Captain Gibbs and Ellie took Miss Tappan, Sadie, Addie, Josie, the dog and I all out sailing. We had a splendid time and were gone from half past two till half past four. We went most up to Tarpaulin Cove.

This afternoon, Miss Tappan, Addie and I went Mayflowering. I got the prettiest ones but I don't think they are plenty at all this year. I went down to Ruth Shiverick's in the evening a little while. The grand Knight of Honor ball is to be a week from today. Frank wrote that if I didn't have an invitation he would take me so guess I shall go. I shall have to wear my new spring dress. It won't be very ballish but it will have to do.

Buzzards Bay shore, March 25, 1881. From the sketchbook of Eva March Tappan. Courtesy WHHC.

THURSDAY, APRIL 21, 1881

Miss Tappan had a letter last night which called her to Boston on business. So there is no school today.

I worked round the house in the morning and in the afternoon I went down to see Emma Hubbard. She has moved into the house Isa Spindel's family have just left. They have gone to Lynn. I had a nice time at Anna's. We went into the new store which is in the basement of the Chapel. It is quite nice there but I think it is a funny place for a store to be. I went down to the train to meet Miss T.

After school I went over to Gracie's a little while. Had a pleasant time. It is not a very pleasant day today. First the sun shines and then it clouds up again.

This evening as the girls went to the sing, Miss Tappan and I went up to Florence's and spent the evening. We ate peanuts all the evening. They invited us to come up every Friday and bring the dog.

We had to have school today as we had a holiday Thursday. After school I had to go up to Cousin Abbie's and have my dress draped. Think I shall like the dress very much but I am almost afraid I shant get the silk for the bodice and tassels in time for the ball. We must send to Jordan Marsh Monday morning.

Ruth Shiverick visited school this morning. I went down there a little while. She was not at home. Papa came home tonight.

Very pleasant but windy. Went to Church morning and evening. Wrote to Myra and studied my German.

Papa did not go today. He is going to stay till Tuesday. We are having a new woodhouse built and the house is being painted. It is a yellow color with green trimmings. Most people don't like it but I do rather. I met Etta this evening and brought her home with me a little while and then Grace came up so we all went to the mail and there met Anna. Etta had to go home but Grace and Anna staid a little while. Went into the store to see Josie who had to tend today.

I don't feel very well today. Hope I shall feel better tomorrow. Ruth Shiverick came up a little while. My cord and tassel and the silk for my dress came this morning.

Almost all the girls are having measles. Isa Norton, Loulie Davis, Katie Donaldson, Lottie Edwards, Alice Grinnell and Persis Crowell all have them.

I am glad I have had them.

The day of the great ball. Studied hard after school and went down to the library a minute. I like my dress very much. Frank came on the train and we went about nine o'clock. Everybody had a nice time. I danced quite a lot but I had not felt very well all day and did not in the evening.

There were a good many strangers there. The supper was nice. I went with Frank. Carrie Rogers and Sam Crowell came to the ball. Papa went today. We got home about half past two.

Rather tired but think I feel better than I did yesterday. Nellie and Frank went to ride this morning and Addie and Fred this afternoon. I felt just like going but of course could not. Carrie Rogers, Nettie and Bessie came in a little while this evening. Everyone but I am tired today. Suppose I shall feel it more tomorrow. Went up to Grandma's a little while.

Rains. The girls, Miss Tappan and I went up to Josie's and spent the evening. We were treated to chocolate caramels. Ellie came in and said Jr. Healey and Jim Duff had had a bad fight and Jim was beaten.

Miss Tappan went to Providence today on business and will return Monday so we will have to make it up Saturday. Went up to Grandma's and helped her and came just before dinner. I worked on my stamp book a while which has been neglected lately. I went over to the store a little while and Fred took me up there and carried to ride down to Quissette and round. Papa did not come home.

Miss Tappan went
to Providence today
on business and will
return Monday so
we will have to
make it up Saturday
Went up to Grand-
ma's and helped her
and came just before
dinner. I worked
on my stamp book
a while which has
been neglected lately.
I went over to the
store a little while and
Fred took me up there
and carried to ride
down to Lysette and
round. Papa did
not come home.

SUNDAY, MAY 1, 1881

...line Smith and
...ill Lewis spent the
...fternoon here, yesterday
...nd Miss Lewis is
...oing to stay over Sunday
Went to Church this
morning and staid
...p to Grandma's till
dinner time and then
...ent again in the eve
...ning. Mr. Henry Dexter
...ame to go Church with
...iss Lennie in the evening.

Celine Smith and Miss Lewis spent the afternoon here yesterday and Miss Lewis is going to stay over Sunday.

Went to Church this morning and staid up to Grandma's till dinner time and then went again in the evening. Mr. Henry Dexter came to go to Church with Miss Lewis in the evening.

No school today. After dinner I went up to see Roy Sturges. They thought yesterday that he had the measles but today they don't think he has. I stayed up there a long while and then went down to Ruth Shiverick's. They think she is coming down with the measles. Miss Tappan came tonight.

Miss Tappan and I went Mayflowering after school and found some lovely ones - the prettiest I have got this year. I will send them to Papa tomorrow.

Went down to Ruthie's a minute after school. I guess she has the measles though not very hard. I heard Minnie Nickerson was sick and went down to see how she was. I guess she is better now but she has been real sick with inflammation of the bowels.

After school Ellie and Fred Gifford took Miss Tappan, Sadie, Ada Poor, Josie and me out sailing. We stayed quite a while. After I got in I heard that Nettie Nickerson had had the measles and had got cold and now she has the pneumonia. He says she is very sick and it is a chance if she gets well again.

Nettie Beach or rather Nettie Thackery came down to the Shiverick's tonight and came here to Bible class. Jimmie Gillingham came here to call on Addie tonight.

Nettie Beach came here to dinner today. She went in the afternoon train. Mr. Fay was here to dinner too. His house is not open and he wanted Mother to board him till tomorrow. It is a horrid rainy day.

Hannah Crowell has the measles and they went to her brain and she has congestion of the brain but I think is a little better than yesterday. Nettie Nickerson is about the same. Ruth Shiverick has the measles in good ernest.

Birdfoot violets, May 13, 1881. From the sketchbook of Eva March Tappan. Courtesy WHHC.

Had to have school today to make up for last Monday. Miss Tappan and I went to walk over to Mr. Fay's for violets and then nearly over to Bay Shore. After I came home I went down to see Ruth Shiverick. She is a little better but she has the real old fashioned measles and is broken out dreadfully. Papa came tonight and Mr. Butler came too.

Went to Church in the morning. Wrote to Lizzie and then Papa. Mother and I went up to Mr. Butler's and all over his place. When I got home Papa was going up to look at Mr. Walsh's pansies so I thought I would go too. When I came home from there, I remembered I had promised Ruth Shiverick to come and see her a minute so I went. After supper, Miss Tappan wanted me to go up to Mr. Butler's with her. Of course I went and then to Church. I never went so much on Sunday before.

Yacht *Mary Lewis* off Cottage City (Oak Bluffs), Martha's Vineyard. Photo by Baldwin Coolidge. Courtesy SPNEA.

Papa went this morning but Mr. Butler will stay till tomorrow. I hear the doctor has pronounced Nettie Nickerson out of danger. This evening I was down to Ruth Shiverick's, who, by the way, is well enough to be down stairs, and Mrs. Shiverick said she heard Anna Hubbard was quite sick with the measles. If it had not been so late I should have gone down then to see how she was.

Miss Tappan, Josie and I went out walking this afternoon.

Fiddle head ferns, May 9, 1881. From the sketchbook of Eva March Tappan. Courtesy WHHC

TUESDAY, MAY 10, 1881

In the afternoon I went over to see Anna. I found she has the measles very badly and a trouble with her throat besides. Guess they feel quite worried about her. Oh! dear me. It seems as if everybody is sick.

On my way home from there, I stopped into Ruthie's. She is crazy to go out but her Mother won't let her.

WEDNESDAY, MAY 11, 1881

After school I went down to Anna's and carried her some pansies. The dr. says she is better but must not get up for three days. This evening, I went down to the library and as Nettie, Addie, Bessie, Sadie, Josie and I were coming home we met Mr. Look and Will Cahoon and Mr. Luscombe met us and wanted us to go down to Quissette to a chowder supper. So we all went just as were. Nettie, Josie and I went with Mr. Luscombe. We had a very nice time and got home about eleven.

"After school I went down to Anna's and carried her some pansies." From the sketchbook of Eva March Tappan. Courtesy WHHC.

THURSDAY, MAY 12, 1881

I have not done much today. We were dreadfully dull at school today and I was awfully sleepy. The girls went to Bible Class in the evening and I studied.

Joseph Story Fay in front of his house, The Homestead, at the head of Little Harbor. Photo by Sarah Bryant Fay. Courtesy WHHC.

This noon Mr. Fay asked us all to go to ride so we hurried through our lessons and went. There were Miss Tappan, Josie, Nellie, Addie and I. Three on a seat. Mr. Fay took us first through the woods and we came out at Devil's Lane and then on we went over the hills a long way and came home another way by the woods. We had a lovely drive and were gone nearly three hours. I went down to Anna's just to inquire after her and in the evening we went out rowing a little while.

Last night Capt. Gibbs asked me to go to No Mans Land with him today so we all got up at half past five and started about six. There were Josie, Miss Tappan, Nellie, Addie and I who went. First we went to Tarpaulin Cove and then to Gay Head and then to No Mans Land where I have never been before. We did not land anywhere but we all had an elegant time. Capt. Gibbs made us eat a second breakfast and then we had dinner, too, on board. We got home about three and Josie had to go to Falmouth so she took me with her. I am pretty tired.

Gay Head from the U.S. Steamer *Verbena*, May 14, 1881. From the sketchbook of Eva March Tappan. Courtesy WHHC.

A horrid stormy day. My face and nose are burned dreadfully. I look as if I had been drinking. I could not go to Church this morning but ventured out in the evening though my face looked awfully.

Tried to write a composition but did not succeed very well.

MONDAY, MAY 16, 1881

Another stormy day. It does not storm all the time but it is foggy when it does not rain. Addie and I went up to Josie's and down to Sadie's a few minutes in the evening.

WEDNESDAY, MAY 18, 1881

Still foggy though it doesn't rain as much as it did yesterday. In the afternoon, I went down to Anna's and carried her some pansies. She is ever so much better and is down stairs. Will Cahoon took me up town by Duff's and brought me home. Then a little while after, I went down to Ruthie's and asked her to spend the day with me tomorrow. Got caught in a shower and had to stop in to Cousin Lyd's. Went down to the library.

Tarpaulin Cove. From the sketchbook of Eva March Tappan. Courtesy WHHC.

Tarpaulin Cove
Lighthouse on
Naushon Island.
Photo by Baldwin
Coolidge, 1896.
Courtesy WHHC.

O dear me! It still rains and I guess it never will stop. Ruth Shiverick did not come till afternoon when it cleared off a little. We walked down to the new store under the chapel and got some candy. Bennie R. is the new clerk there. He feels quite big.

Henry Fay's yacht in her winter covering. From the sketchbook of Eva March Tappan. Courtesy WHHC.

FRIDAY, MAY 20, 1881

It was a little foggy in the morning and evening but in the afternoon it was quite pleasant. Miss T. and I went to walk over to Mr. Glidden's to paint his old house.

We found the first buttercups of the season. When we came home, we stopped for Miss T. to draw Henry Fay's yacht in her winter covering. While I was waiting, I found my first four leaved clover. Papa came home tonight sick. He does not really know what ails him.

SATURDAY, MAY 21, 1881

A pleasant day at last. Went up to Grandma's in the morning and stayed till dinner time. The doctor came to see Papa in the afternoon.

He has broken a small artery in his head and it makes him deaf but thinks he will get well all right. Went over to Grace's in the afternoon and we went to walk a little way.

Went down to the library in the evening.

Pleasant. Went to Church all day. The sack to my new dress is finished and I wore it. Almost everybody had on new hats. Josie, Florence, Addie, Bessie, Nettie, Ruth, Charrie Purdum and Abbie.

The dr. came to Papa and he says he may always be deaf but he feels better today.

This recess Ellie and I went out rowing. We do very often when it is pleasant. He always carries something good to eat. We started to go out sailing but did not hardly get out of the harbor because there was no wind. We walked down to Bar Neck to pay the washer-woman. Ruth Shiverick came up in the evening.

Ellie and I went out rowing at recess. The doctor came today and said Papa was much better. He brought another doctor with him. I guess they had been to Mrs. Grinnell who is very sick with pneumonia.

Miss Tappan and I went to walk over to the old orchard and Miss Tappan drew the old duckhouse back of Emma Edwards and I made my first sketch of a pair of bars.

Went down to the library in the evening and then Gracie and I went up to Minnie

Four-leaf clover pressed in the diary on May 20, 1881.

Robinson's a few minutes. They are expecting Willie home every day now. Hope he will come soon for Minnie looks dreadfully.

THURSDAY, MAY 26, 1881

This noon Josie asked me to go to the circus at Falmouth with her this afternoon so I went of course. Miss Tappan and Ellie went too. It was the first circus I have ever been too. Liked it pretty well but there were not hardly anyone there. About all were 80 yrs. and children.

FRIDAY, MAY 27, 1881

I am rather tired today. Didn't do much all day. All most got to sleep in the evening but Miss Tappan wanted me to go to Josie's with her so I went.

SATURDAY, MAY 28, 1881

Went up to Grandma's awhile and helped her then came home and put stamps in my book.

On my way to Grandma's I saw Mary Davis and she said Isa was sick again and her mother went this morning. They don't know whether it is the measles or not. I hope she is not very sick.

Went down to the library this evening and met Gracie. Addie had a May basket tonight and we chased till quite late.

Old Duck house, May 25, 1881. From the sketchbook of Eva March Tappan. Courtesy WHHC.

Went to Church all day and studied in the afternoon. Ought to have written a composition but did not. I think some of going to Barnum's Circus over to New Bedford. Two circuses in one week! But I thought as Ruthie Shiverick was going I might for perhaps I shall not be at home another year. Guess Addie will go too and Nettie and Bessie.

Got up quite early and found it pleasant. Addie and I started down to Shiverick's and found Bessie and Ruth both sick so they could not go. We were very sorry but it could not be helped so Mr. Shiverick, Persis, Nettie, Addie and I went. We shopped some in the morning, dined at the Bancroft House and then went to the circus. I liked it very much. It beats Falmouth all to smash. We saw the baby elephant, Chang the giant, Tom Thumb and his wife and everything else. Think the riding was the best. Met Lizzie and L. Babcock. We got an ice cream afterwards.

I am very tired today but am glad I went. Gracie went with Mr. Thrasher who keeps the new store.

I lay down all this afternoon but could not get to sleep. Went out rowing in the evening and took Miss Kelly, Mrs. Davis' girl. Elmer Donaldson came home yesterday and I saw him today. He is raising side whiskers. I did not know him.

I am about as tired toda
as I was yesterday,
After supper I went
down to Anna Hubbard
and asked her to spend
to day with me tomorrow
I came home a little
before nine and then
the boys bring some can
dy here and I had to
Chase of course. Suppose
it was a June box,

June

Emma did not come.
Miss Kelly and I went
out rowing in the
evening.

I am about as tired today as I was yesterday.

After supper, I went down to Anna Hubbard's and asked her to spend today with me tomorrow. I came home a little before nine and then the boys hung some candy here and I had to chase, of course. Suppose it was a June box.

Anna did not come. Miss Kelly and I went out rowing in the evening.

Miss T. and I went up to Josie's in the evening.

Rains. Went up to Grandma's and worked all the morning. Stayed to dinner there. In the afternoon about four o'clock, it cleared off and I went rowing.

It was very still so I rowed over to Nobsque, landed and went up to Nettie Nickerson's a few minutes. When I got down to the shore, the boat was stuck and it took me a long while to get it off. I got home and they were waiting supper for me.

Papa doesn't want me to land there anymore.

Went to Church. Studied my German, wrote to Lizzie and read a little in "Countess Gisela".

Spring flowers.
From the sketch-
book of Eva
March Tappan.
Courtesy WHHC.

Shore where Ruth
Anna's rowboat got
stuck. Nobska
Lighthouse, Henry
Fay water tower
and house in back-
ground. Courtesy
WHHC.

I ought to have written a composition but of course I did not. Went to Church in the evening.

MONDAY, JUNE 6, 1881

After school, Miss T. and I went to walk. We only went as far as Sam Wing's field on the track. Miss Tappan sketched this side of the railroad bridge, the old willow tree and Sturgis' house. I read and tried to write my composition in the evening.

Papa went today. We did not want him to but he would.

TUESDAY, JUNE 7, 1881

Not very pleasant. Went down to Anna's and asked her to come up and see me one day this week. I don't know what day she will come. When I came home I stopped into Ruth Shiverick's a few minutes. Stayed at home in the evening.

Minnie Robinson is quite bad. They are expecting Willie home now every day. Hope he will get here so that Minnie may see him. I broke my glasses today while fooling with Ellie. Sent them right out to Boston.

Church Street bridge with Reuben Hamlin farm on right, Simeon Hamlin farm on left, June 6, 1881. From the sketchbook of Eva March Tappan. Courtesy WHHC.

It rains. It cleared off partly about three o'clock and I bailed the boat out and went out rowing. After supper, Miss Kelly came for me to go to the library so I went and then we went out rowing. It was cloudy but just as still as it could be. We did not come in till nine o'clock. Anna did not come because it was not pleasant.

We have a postal from Papa every night. Says he is getting along nicely.

Josie asked Miss Tappan and I to come up and spend the afternoon because her father, grandmother and Uncle Charles had gone down to their Aunt Josephine's. Miss Tappan had to go home early in the evening and when I got ready to go home it rained so hard that they made me stay all night. Josie and I studied in the evening.

Real penny post
cards from Woods
Holl, Mass.
Courtesy WHHC.

I came home about half past seven in time to get a second breakfast.

It is an awful day. It is a perfect gale and rains pouring.

Anna did not come of course. It seems as if I was fated to get her up here. I asked her to come last week but she could not. Josie stayed and spent the day.

Nellie went up to Grandma's and I stayed at home and helped do housework. Went down to Ruth Shiverick's a little while in the afternoon. Miss Kelly and I went out rowing and Ellie came out and brought a lot of candy and some oranges. We had a nice time.

Papa came tonight. The Shivericks were expecting Charlie and his family tonight but they did not come. Papa brought my glasses.

Went to Church and Miss Kelly went with me. Wrote no letters. Read a little and went to Church in the evening.

Not very pleasant. Gracie came in the evening and stayed awhile.

I went down to Ruth Shiverick's a minute this P.M. and then went into Gertrude's. She was so glad to see me that she made me stay to tea. I played house and told stories and played school, and I guess she had a good time. Guess it will clear off tomorrow.

Anna came this afternoon. We went in and called on Grace Kelly and we went out rowing a few minutes after supper. After she went home, Sadie, Ellie and I went rowing. It was lovely.

The last day of school. I am very glad. Miss Tappan is going up to Josie's to spend a week and Jennie Grant is coming there tomorrow. Then Miss Tappan is going to the Quissette Harbor House for a month. Charlie Shiverick and his family came this noon.

Nellie went to New Bedford with Miss Tappan and Jennie Grant came. I worked all the morning and part of the afternoon on my room and I can't make it look nice at all. Miss K. and I went rowing in the evening. Minnie Robinson is failing fast. I wish Willie would come. Gertrude spent the day with me. Mrs. Bolles had a son today.

Went up to Grandma's and worked. I got an old fashioned wash stand up there and Papa has varnished it so that it looks splendid. It is the prettiest thing in my room. It is Papa's birthday today. He is fifty nine years old. We gave him an individual castor with a napkin ring attached. Cousin Charles gave him a handkerchief and Mr. Messer a bushel of potatoes. Grandma spent the afternoon and Cousin Abbie, Sadie, Add, Will C., Fred and I went out rowing.

Frank came last night. I went to Church as usual in the morning and evening. Stayed on the piazza most of the afternoon. Wrote to Isa Poor. We heard this noon that Mr. Robinson saw a barque come in that looked like Willie's so he, Madison and Ephraim Edwards went out in their boat to bring him home for Minnie is very low. I watched all that afternoon for them but they did not get home till nine o'clock. We were on the piazza and saw him go past.

Papa worked all the morning and part of the afternoon, cutting over a bedstead for my room. He has made it into a single bedstead and it is real nice. I helped him and got real tired.

Brin Eldridge came this noon but he stays at Aunt Mahala's. I stayed at home all the afternoon. I broke my glasses for the 2nd time this afternoon.

Mr. and Mrs. Carleton have gone up to John's graduation. He graduates this week.

I think I shall go to New Bedford Friday and stay a week. I have got to have my teeth filled as usual. I mean to come home before the fourth.

Nettie Shiverick came up a while this morning and brought her little nephew Asa with her. He is about four I should think. I like him and he has taken quite a fancy to me. I went down there a little while in the evening and saw the other two children. George Eldridge came today.

WEDNESDAY, JUNE 22, 1881

Papa went this morning. It seems lonesome without him. Louise Butler came Saturday and I went up to call on her today. Had a pleasant call. I had a letter from Isa Poor and Lizzie today. Lizzie wants Ruth Shiverick and I to come over and spend the fourth. I did not want to go there the fourth but I shall have to, for Ruth's school wont be out till the Friday before. Went down to hall and got ice cream in the evening. They are going to have it there once a week all summer.

THURSDAY, JUNE 23, 1881

A.M. Went up to Grandma's a few minutes. Sadie and Nellie Taylor who is visiting her, came here to spend the day. P.M. Stayed at home and after tea, Gracie came up and then we went over to her house and swung in her hammock.

I am trying to decide what school to go to next fall. I have about decided to go to Andover.* I had a catalogue from there yesterday.

Liberty Hall, built in 1878 for community meetings and entertainments, as seen from Great Harbor. The old stone bridge was built over the Channel into Eel Pond in 1878. Courtesy WHHC.

* Abbot Academy in Andover

Went up Fislie a few moments this A.M. *Went down to Anna's and stayed all the afternoon. We played croquet. I met Grace on the street and went over there to swing in her hammock.*

Saw Willie Robinson for the first time tonight. He seems just the same as ever. There is a comet* to be seen now. We looked at it tonight.

* The Great Comet of 1881

Mother and Addie went to Boston this morning and came home with Papa tonight. I helped Nellie a long while and then went up to Grandma's and helped her.

P.M. *Emma Edwards came up to see me and stayed all the afternoon. Went down to the library.*

Went to Church both morning and evening. Had a very hard shower while we were at Church in the evening.

Read "Old Myddleton's Money" this P.M.

Miss Tappan and Jennie Grant came here to stay a few days today. Josie, Florence and Ellie spent the day. Lizzie wants me to come over there tomorrow so as to see the great wedding which is to be there Wednesday but as I had decided to go Thursday, I guess I shall wait and go then. Ruth S. is going Saturday.

Nothing special doing today. The Shiverick family came for a few minutes this evening.

Not very pleasant. Nothing going on all day.

The Shivericks came in this evening again on an errand and stayed some time.

Jo, Miss T., Jennie and Nellie went to the Vineyard today but we all went sailing first and stayed quite a while. I worked all the rest of the morning and ironed till after three. Addie and I went to a dance in the evening and had a nice time. Jenn and Miss T. would not go so we were not going but they teazed us so and went to ride themselves, so we thought we might as well go.

Steamer *Sankaty* leaving Woods Hole Town Wharf. Travel by boat between Woods Hole and New Bedford was convenient and inexpensive. Courtesy WHHC.

Pleasant. Went to New Bedford by boat. Carl met me there. Then I went to Dr. McLeod's and had one tooth filled. He almost killed me. Then I went over to Fair Haven to dinner and at two o'clock went to the dr.'s and had two more teeth filled. That is all there is to be done this time over. Went to bed early this evening for I am awfully tired.

A picnic at the fort.
It was got up by the
High School scholars.
We had a magnific-
ent time. Wore in
white dress. There is
a pavillion on the
grounds and we dan
all the afternoon and
evening without any
music. The pavillion
has a splendid floor
for dancing. I got
acquainted with lots
of nice girls. Say Allen
Sue Damon, Minnie
Keith and lots of other
We did not get home
till half past nine

SATURDAY, JULY 2, 1881

We went over to New
Bedford and met
with S. Shiverick and
came right home. A most
awful thing happened
today. This noon we
were out in front of the
house eating cherries
when suddenly all the
church bells began to
toll. Aunt Sarah said something
awful must have happened
she said, but did not really
think so, that perhaps Garfield was dead, The first
man who came along we
asked what was the matter.
He said "Garfield is dead - shot",
never felt any worse in my life.
Soon we heard he was not-

but fatally injured

dead

A picnic at the Fort. It was got up by the High School scholars. We had a magnificent time. Wore my white dress. There is a pavilion on the grounds and we danced all afternoon and evening without any music. The pavillion has a splendid floor for dancing. I got acquainted with lots of nice girls. Say Allen, Sue Damon, Minnie Keith and lots of others. We did not get home till half past nine.

We went over to New Bedford and met Ruth Shiverick and came right home. A most awful thing happened today. This noon we were out in front of the house eatting cherries when suddenly all the Church bells began to toll. Aunt Sarah said something awful must have happened. I said, but did not really think so, that perhaps Garfield was dead. The first man who came along, we asked what was the matter. He said, "Garfield is dead - shot". I never felt any worse in my life. Soon we heard he was not dead but fatally injured, and then that perhaps he might live.

Penikese Island, from the U.S. Steamer *Verbena,* July 2, 1881. From the sketchbook of Eva March Tappan. Courtesty WHHC.

The first thing we heard was that Garfield was dead. Then a man with a paper came along and they said he was better. You can't seem to tell anything about it. We don't know whether the fourth will be celebrated or not. I felt dreadfully yesterday but felt a little better about it today. We went to Sabbath School this A.M., meeting this afternoon and a floral concert this P.M. We went to bed early. Emma Eldreds brother Davis came here last night.

MONDAY, JULY 4, 1881

The bells rung this morning so we knew the immortal fourth would be celebrated. We got up half past four, missed the horse car walked the bridge and saw the horribles. They were not so good as they were last fourth.

We came home, lay down, went to sleep and slept till ten. Then we got up and went over to see the G.A.R. procession. It had just begun when news came that Garfield was dying and so there was no more celebration. We came home but got some ice cream first and went down to Card's in the afternoon and got some more. Afterwards we heard it was a false alarm about the President dying. We stayed at home in the. P.M.

TUESDAY, JULY 5, 1881

Garfield is no worse this morning or at least there was no bad news about him. I have been thinking of him all the time ever since I heard of the terrible thing. I wonder if Arthur or Conkling had anything to do with it! I can't think they did. I went over to N.B. this afternoon and what do you think, I did. I had

my picture taken. My Mother has been teazing
me for a long while to have it done so I did. We
did some shopping and got some ice cream.
Mattie and Annie Wilkie came in this evening.

WEDNESDAY, JULY 6, 1881

It is an awful hot day. We wanted to see the
cemetery before we went home so we three went
up there this morning. It is almost two miles
there and it was awful hot. When we got home
we lay down and rested awhile. We did not do
anything in particular the rest of the day.
Panlis has been here on a visit and yesterday he
went to W.H. to see Ellie. Guess we will go home
tomorrow.

THURSDAY, JULY 7, 1881

Quissett roses, July
13, 1881. From the
sketchbook of Eva
March Tappan.
Courtesy WHHC.

We packed this morning. The proofs of my
pictures came this noon. One of them is quite
good but I think it flatters a little. We started
over to N.B. about three because we had little
shopping to do. The boat started at four and we
got home at six. No one was expecting us and
I walked into the sitting room before they saw
me. Went up to Grandma's after supper. Met
Anna and walked down a little way with her.

FRIDAY, JULY 8, 1881

Went to Mrs. Benj. Gifford's to carry her some
roses. I stayed a little while and then went to
carry Anna some. Stopped into Shiverick's
when I was coming home. Went out rowing
with Lewis Clarke in the afternoon. Harry

Butler came in stayed quite a while so I had to entertain two young gentlemen. Miss Kelly's brother is here so Ruth S. and I took them out rowing after tea.

SATURDAY, JULY 9, 1881

I stayed at home this morning and Addie went up to Grandma's. George Eldridge came to-night and brought his girl, Eaddie Shaw with him to spend Sunday. Papa came tonight. Miss Shaw, Addie and I went out rowing and Carlie and Ellie went and they plagued us so that we had to come in. Afterwards they brought me half a dozen pickle limes as a peace offering. I took a music lesson today. Like John Swift ever so much.

SUNDAY, JULY 10, 1881

Went to Church A.M. *and* P.M. *Stayed to lunch down to Shiverick's. Carl came in to dinner and went to Brockton on the evening train.*

MONDAY, JULY 11, 1881

George and Miss Shaw and Papa went this morning. Not very pleasant all day.

TUESDAY, JULY 12, 1881

Very dull today. Did not do anything but work and practise.

Went down to the hall this evening and got ice cream. Mrs. Luscombe took the whole crowd in. Harry Butler came in and stayed most all the afternoon. My pictures came tonight.

Very warm today. Had my white dress on all day. Isa Poor came tonight. Miss Kelly and I went down to Anna's and stayed all the evening.

Minnie Robinson died today. It was this afternoon at nearly night.

Went to Grandma's and helped her. Took my music lesson in the afternoon. Papa came tonight.

Did not feel well so did not go to Church this A.M. Went to the hall with Ruth in the evening.

Gertrude came in this morning and stayed till after dinner. Minnie Robinson's funeral was in the Chapel this afternoon. I went but did not see her because Nero came in and I had to carry him home. It rained most all the afternoon and evening.

Quissett Harbor
with Harbor
House on left in
background.
Photo by Baldwin
Coolidge, 1897.
Courtesy WHHC.

Mr. Messer,
conductor on the
Dude Train.
Courtesy WHHC.

Did not do anything till after dinner. Harry came and asked us all to go out sailing in the "Julia". Nellie, Miss Blandin and I went. Addie was sick. We had an elegant time and went just in sight of Nantucket which I have never seen before. We got home about seven and had a lovely breeze all the way. Isa Poor, Ruth S. and I went out rowing in the evening.

Last night Mr. Messer invited Ruth S., Persis Crowell and I to go to Boston with him today so we went. We went both ways in the palace car. Mr. M. took us up in the Equitable Building and then we went down to Papa's store. We came home in the three o'clock train.

In the evening we went to hear "Uncle Tom's Cabin" at the hall. Of course it was not so good as you would hear in the city but it was good for Wood's Holl.

All ready for a
swim in Quissett
Harbor. From
the sketch-book
of Eva March
Tappan. Courtesy
WHHC.

Had a hard tempest this morning and it was squally all day. It cleared off lovely in the evening and we went out rowing. Uncle Tim went to Boston today on the "Julia" and Grandma came here to stay till he comes back. Aunt Sarah and Lizz are coming next week.

This morning, Ruth Shiverick came up and asked Addie and I to go out sailing and see the school ship but it went before we got there so we went to the Quissette Harbor House and saw Miss Tappan. We got becalmed on the way home and had to go without our dinner till after two o'clock.

SATURDAY, JULY 23, 1881

John Swift did not come to give me a lesson. He has a fish bone in his hand. I suppose that is the reason. Went out rowing this morning.

SUNDAY, JULY 24, 1881

Did not go to Church this morning. I don't feel very well lately. I get tired even if I do nothing. Went in the evening to Church. There were more people out this morning than any Sunday this Summer.

Mr. Carleton is going to resign in October. Guess he will go down to Sandwich on John's farm.

Quissett Harbor House, August 8, 1881. From the sketchbook of Eva March Tappan. Courtesy WHHC.

MONDAY, JULY 25, 1881

I feel badly today.

Ellie and Isa Poor came for me to go to hear "Comical Brown" tonight. I went but did not like it very well though we had fun.

Isa came in for me to go down to call on Miss Chapman. She is Mr. Chapman's, the cook at the factory's, sister. I did not feel very well so I told her I would not go. I have never been introduced to Miss Chapman but have seen her. She is very pretty and stylish.

Josie, Sadie and Addie were going to the hall to see "Enock Arden" played so I thought I would go. It was very good indeed. Nellie went to New Bedford today to have her teeth filled.

Nellie came in the afternoon boat. Went down to the hall this evening to get ice cream. Was introduced to Miss Chapman. Like her very much though I only saw her a short time. Isa did not call on her till this afternoon because it was stormy yesterday.

A very hot day. Isa, Anna and I were out rowing in the evening.

Probably Edward G. Gardiner, one of the founders, in 1888, of the MBL

Early this afternoon Mr. Gardiner, * a gentleman who lodges here invited us to go out fishing. The girls could not go so I got Isa Poor to go. We had a splendid time and did not get home till nearly 7 'clock. Mr. Gardiner had a friend with him, Mr. Trelise (I can't spell it). He was nice but very funny. We caught lots of fish.

SATURDAY, JULY 30, 1881

Went up Grandma's and came home before dinner. Waited all the afternoon for John Swift to give me my music lesson but he did not come. Guess he forgot it. Mother finished my white dress so that I can wear it tomorrow if it is pleasant.

Nellie's is done too. I went down to Anna's a few minutes after tea.

SUNDAY, JULY 31, 1881

A hot day and sometimes it rains a little. Went to Church morning and evening. Mr. Gardiner went with me in the A.M. Could not wear my white dress because it did not look as it would be pleasant in the morning. I am reading "Dombey and Son". Like it very much but it takes a long time to read it.

A hot day and sometime
it rains a little.
Went to Church
morning and evening
Mr. Gardiner went
with me in the A.M.
Could not wear my white
dress because it did
not look as if it would
be pleasant in the
morning. I am reading
"Dombey and Son".
Like it very much
but it takes a long
time to read it.

MONDAY, AUGUST 1, 1881

...oggy. Went down to
...ns Kelly's a few minutes
...ae P.M. She is not
...ry well today. Mr. Gar-
...ner asked us to go
...t fishing. Nellie, Add,
...nd I went. Addie and
...each caught a blue
...ish. It was our first-
...e, too. We did not-
...et home till eight
...clock. Mr. Gardiner
...ot supper here.

U. S. Fish Com-
mission steamer
Fish Hawk.
Photo by Baldwin
Coolidge. Courtesy
WHHC.

MONDAY, AUGUST 1, 1881

*Foggy. Went down to Sim Kelly's a few min-
utes this P.M. She is not very well today. Mr.
Gardiner asked us to go out fishing. Nellie,
Add and I went. Addie and I caught a blue
fish. It was our first one, too. We did not get
home till eight o'clock. Mr. Gardiner got
supper here.*

TUESDAY, AUGUST 2, 1881

*Not pleasant until nearly night. After it cleared
off, I went down and called on Miss Chapman.
I had a splendid time. She is very pleasant.
After tea, Isa came and asked me to go down
on board the Fish Hawk, - Professor Beard's
steamer. Miss Chapman went too. We had a
lovely time on board. It is a splendid steamer.*

WEDNESDAY, AUGUST 3, 1881

*We expected Lizzie here today but she did not
come. Went down to the hall to get ice cream.
Miss Chapman was there.*

*Mr. Gardiner took Addie and I sailing up to
Hadley Harbor. It was beautiful there.*

THURSDAY, AUGUST 4, 1881

*Lizzie did come today. We went out rowing in
the evening. It was lovely on the water.*

FRIDAY, AUGUST 5, 1881

*I went down to Sadie's this morning and
learned how to make rick-rack trimming.*

Hadley Harbor,
August 30, 1897.
Photo by Baldwin
Coolidge. Courtesy
WHHC.

Lizzie and I are invited down to Isa's tomorrow to spend the afternoon. Miss Chapman is invited. It is a horrid feeling day. I went to bed very early.

SATURDAY, AUGUST 6, 1881

Lizzie and I went down to Isa's about four o'clock. We played on the piano almost all the afternoon. Miss C. sang to us. In the evening a gentleman on the Fish Hawk called and we had more music. Papa came home tonight. I had a letter from Miss Tappan tonight. It is about my going away to school. I am pretty sure I shall go to Abbot Academy at Andover.

SUNDAY, AUGUST 7, 1881

Not very pleasant. This is the second Sunday that I have not been able to wear my white dress. We went down to the hall in the evening.

MONDAY, AUGUST 8, 1881

Papa went this morning. Isa, Lizzie, Lizzie Chapman and myself went over to the light house this morning. We did not get back till after twelve.

We had an invitation to go sailing on the Julia but we did not go. After tea, Ellie invited Isa Poor, Lizzie and I to go to ride. We had a splendid time. Got home about half past nine.

Eating bread and butter on the yacht *Dawn*, August 8, 1881. From the sketchbook of Eva March Tappan. Courtesy WHHC.

Mr. Gardiner asked us all to go out fishing this morning. It was our last chance as he was going this P.M. Nellie and I went.

Mr. Trelease went too. They all caught a blue fish but me. Just as I was coming in, I felt an awful pull at my line and it was a long time before I could move it. But after a while, I pulled the fish way up to the boat and was going to land it when the line broke. They said the fish must have weighed at least ten pounds.

I got a letter from Miss McKeen the principal of Abbot Academy tonight. She sent me a credential for Miss Tappan to sign and then I shant have to pass an examination. We went down to the hall to get ice cream and then we went out rowing.

Mother went to N.B. today and brought me home a gingham dress and green flannel and lots of other things.

Lizz and I went down to Anna's this evening. I am going to have company tomorrow - Anna, Isa, Gracie, Ruth S. and Julia Rankin who is visiting at Gracie's.

We stayed all night last night at Gramma's. All my company came this afternoon. We had

Fishing from the yacht *Wild Maria*, Quissett, August 23, 1881. From the sketchbook of Eva March Tappan. Courtesy WHHC.

a pleasant time but it was hard to find any-thing to entertain them with. It was Anna's birthday today. She is sixteen.

Grandma came here today to stay a while. Aunt Sarah is here.

SATURDAY, AUGUST 13, 1881

I wrote to Miss Tappan today and asked her and her mother to spend the day here Tuesday. Then I can see her about going away to school.

Papa came tonight. I went down to Isa's a little while to show her how to make rick-rack trimming.

SUNDAY, AUGUST 14, 1881

Mr. and Mrs. Carleton have gone to Vermont on a vacation and Mr. Gibson from Baltimore preached today. Did not like him very well. Mr. Converse preached last Sunday. Isa Poor went to Church with us this morning.

MONDAY, AUGUST 15, 1881

Mother began my green flannel today. Lizzie, Isa and I went out rowing this evening. By and by Harry Butler and Ellie came along in their sailboat. Harry got into our boat and by and by I got into Ellie's boat. We went around the harbor quite a while and had a jolly time.

TUESDAY, AUGUST 16, 1881

I had to go down to Quissette Harbor House this morning after Mrs. and Miss Tappan to spend the day. Miss T. had gone to New Bedford but she came on the noon boat. She signed my credential. Lizzie, Isa and I went out rowing a while and Ellie towed us in his sail boat. I could not stay so long as the rest because Miss T. was here.

Two weeks from today I go away to school. I don't know whether I want to go or not. It is a horrid storm. Lizzie went up to Grandma's and did not come for all day. I went down to the library in the evening.

Lizzie and I went down to Isa's this afternoon and then again in the eve. We made molasses candy and danced. Isa only knows how to dance a little so we tried to show her. We heard John Carleton had shot his hand quite badly. He may lose the use of it.

I don't feel very well. Lizzie and I were going down to Anna's but it has been stormy all the week and I don't feel well today so guess we shant get there this week. Isa came in a few minutes this afternoon and she and Ruth S. spent the evening here. Ruth invited Lizzie and I to see her tomorrow afternoon.

John Carleton's hand is not so bad as we heard it was but he may lose his little finger.

SATURDAY, AUGUST 20, 1881

This morning I had a note from Anna wanting us to come and see her this P.M. but we could not go as we were going to Ruth's.

About noon I had a note from Louise asking us to take a drive down to Falmouth. I did want to go very much but of course I could not. We had a very good time at Ruth's. Papa came tonight.

SUNDAY, AUGUST 21, 1881

Lizzie and I went to Church this morning and evening. We stayed to lunch at Cousin Abbie's. A Mr. Gushie preached here today.

MONDAY, AUGUST 22, 1881

Lizzie Maybury, a friend of Sadie's and Sadie spent the day here with Addie. Maggie Roland from Norfolk came up to see Cousin Abbie and she was not at home so she came to our house to tea. Anna asked Lizzie and I to spend the afternoon there tomorrow. Isa, Lizzie and I went out rowing and Harry and Ellie were out. They were towing us when we bumped into them so hard that our lantern fell out and broke.

TUESDAY, AUGUST 23, 1881

We went down to Anna's and had a very nice time. Isa was there.

I went over to call on Grace and Julia Rankin today because I heard they were going tomorrow and I should not see them again very soon. But they are not going till Saturday. A week from today I go away to school. Don't know whether I want to go or not.

Mr. Hill came today. Guess he came to see Add. Anyway, he is in here all the time.

This morning I woke up with something the matter with my eye. It seems like a distemper. It was better at night and I was glad because there was a dance at night and I wanted to go. We all went and had a pretty good time but it was rather dull.

Louise came for Lizzie and I to go to ride this afternoon. We went over Beebe's place and down the shore road through Falmouth. Ruth Basset, a friend of Louise's went too. This morning Mrs. Mary Gifford invited us girls down there to tea at half past six. Nellie and I went and had a splendid time. The captain of an Italian barque and a little boy called in the evening. They could speak but very little English.

Following page:
The garden at the
"Beebe's place,"
Highfield, Falmouth.
Courtesy Falmouth
Historical Society.

Lizzie went today. I went down to the library in the evening. We were up to Louise Butler's this morning.

Mr. Converse preached today and the Little Wanderers were here in the afternoon. It is my last Sunday at home.

I have got something the matter with my eyes again. I don't know what it can be. This (morning) Mr. Poor came for me to go out in the steam launch but I was not ready and I looked too bad so I would not go. But I wanted to go awfully. This evening, Isa and her cousin Ida Tarbox who is visiting her came for me to go out rowing this evening, so I went. We had a nice time. It may be my last row for this summer.

I heard this morning that Isa was sick - that she had a hemorhage in the night. I was going down to see her the first thing in the afternoon but Louise, Ruth and Olive Morrison came and stayed till most five. Then I went down and found her in bed on the lounge. She felt badly when I came away. Then I went around making my farewell calls. In the P. M. Ellie came for me to go to drive. We went to see Miss Tappan and down to Falmouth.

The great day has arrived. Mother, Nell and I started on the first train leaving Add to keep house. Papa met us in Boston and we took the 12 M. train to Andover. Got here about one. Was happily disappointed in the place. My room is very pleasant and so is my roommate, Hattie Clarke. Like Miss Brownell. It is an awful hot day.

Mother and Nell went to the Mansion House to stay all night.

Woods Hole Railroad Station. Ruth Anna took the train to Boston and then on to Andover for her schooling at Abbot Academy. Courtesy WHHC.

Student's room at Abbot Academy in the 1880s. Courtesy Phillips Academy.

Another awfull hot
day. Mother and Nell
came to say good bye
this morning. It seemed
bad to have them go.
We went to the hall
at nine to have our
names taken and
studies assigned.
Did not do much
studying this ~~morn~~
evening. I wore my
new gingham today.
Like it very much.

Sept

FRIDAY, SEPTEMBER 2, 1881

rain storm and rather
d. I went to see Miss
M. Keen about my
studies and she said
ould not graduate in
three years and that
must take English
istry and Physiology
v. I went and told
iss Brownell and I
ied because I was
homesick. She went
see Miss Mc. Keen and
alked to her so that
guess, if I study hard
can graduate in three
ars. I have got to take
ivate lessons in Latin
f Miss Hall. It will cost
fifty cents a lesson.

Another awfully hot day. Mother and Nell came to say goodbye this morning. It seemed sad to have them go. We went to the hall at nine to have our names taken and studies assigned. Did not do much studying this evening. I wore my new gingham today. Like it very much.

A rain storm and rather cold. I went to see Miss McKeen about my studies and she said I could not graduate in three years and that I must take English, History and Physiology over. I went and told Miss Brownell and I cried because I was homesick. She went to see Miss McKeen and talked to her so that I guess, if I study hard I can graduate in three years. I have got to take private lessons in Latin of Miss Hall. It will cost fifty cents a lesson. A letter from Addie.

Yesterday I went with my roommate to see her mother at Mrs. Eaton's. I did not think of asking permission and when I got back at the supper table, Miss B. asked me where I had been. I told her very innocently and how the girls laughed at me! Studied this morning.

This afternoon Miss McKeen gave out rules and one of them was that you can't write but one letter on Sunday. I don't know what I shall do. I had a letter from home and Lizzie.

We went to the Congregationalist Church. Mother went to ask Miss McKeen if I could go to the Episcopal Church and she would not let me. Before lunch I went over to the library and got a book. Hattie went up to see her mother and Mary Gorton came to see me. Generally they don't allow the girls to have company Sunday afternoon. I wrote a long letter home. Right after supper there is an hour that we are allowed to go visiting in. We divide it into quarters. I spent mine with Lucy Clarke, Marion Keene, Lois Warner and Emily Mather.

We engage a different walker for every day in the week. Today I walked Lily Fahnstock. We have to walk twice every day. This afternoon we walked down street. Monday evenings, the girls have a prayer meeting in the music room. I had a letter from Louise today and from home. Letters are good.

This morning I was to walk with Mary Hillard but she forgot it so I walked with Carrie Puffer, one of the Smith Hall girls. This afternoon I walked with Mary Gorton. We took a long walk through the Willows and by the Theological Seminary.

I am having a hard time in my Virgil and I study Phys. Geog. The books have not come

Abbot Hall, main
classroom building,
Abbot Academy.
Courtesy Phillips
Academy.

Main residence,
Smith Hall, Abbot
Academy, 1888.
Courtesy Phillips
Academy.

General campus,
Abbot Academy,
1888. Courtesy
Phillips Academy.

and I have to borrow one to study out of so I don't get my lessons very well. I had a letter from Papa with some stamps.

Another hot day. Hattie swept the room today because she wants to go to Boston next week. I washed quite a number of things and ironed them. Miss Peabody is my walker today. I went up in her room and there were lots of girls there. I stayed a while and then we went to walk. We had to study this evening.

Matie Kuhnen and I walked this morning way down almost out of town. It was a nice walk. Lois Warner and I took a short walk this afternoon down in the grove. Then Hattie and I took a walk almost down to town.

I walked with Marion Keene this afternoon. We went to Rabbitt's pond and Missionary Grove. Had a nice time. In the five o'clock study hour, Mrs. Gorton told me that I had a caller. It was Mrs. Nutting. Miss Perkins asked her to call on me. I had a nice call and she asked me to go to ride with her tomorrow and to go to tea. I know I can't go to tea there but I guess I can go ride.

Not very pleasant. I am afraid Mrs. Nutting will not come for me to go to drive. Took my first Latin lesson of Miss Hall this morning. Like her very much. I waited for Mrs. Nutting this afternoon till nearly five and then concluded she was not coming so went down town with Hattie. I met her on the way coming for me. She thought I was free till six o'clock. She said she would take me Tuesday and then I could stay to tea. A letter from home.

This morning Miss B. sent me over to ask Miss McK. if I could not go to the Episcopal Church with her this morning. She let me but she did not want to. The Church is not very pretty but it seemed like home and I felt rather homesick, when I first went in. Annie Peabody and Lois Warner go to the Episcopal Church. It is not very pleasant today. I wrote home. Spent my quarters with Mary Decker, Mary Hillard, Lois Warner and Julia Spear.

A letter from home. Lily Fahnestock was sick so I did not walk with her today.

I expected Mrs. Nutting all the afternoon but she did not come at all nor send any word. I was quite disappointed but just as I had given her up, Mary Gorton came and told me that I

Tennis at Abbot
Academy in the
1880s. Courtesy
Phillips Academy.

*had an express box downstairs. I flew down
stairs and found quite a large box from Papa.
It contained a nice student lamp and some
peaches and bananas and a fruit dish I had
sent for. About the same time I got a nice box
of flowers from home.*

WEDNESDAY, SEPTEMBER 14, 1881

*Hattie went to Boston today. She went before
breakfast and came home just before supper. I
swept and washed and ironed and recited my
Latin lessons to Miss Hall. When Hattie came
back she brought a table cover, a splasher and
some grapes. Guess she had a good time.*

THURSDAY, SEPTEMBER 15, 1881

*This afternoon, Lois Warner and I took quite
a long walk. We went on the streets back of the
Acad. and we were walking on a street we had
never been on before when I looked up and
found we were right opposite one of the dormi-
tories. We just turned around rather quick.*

I was walking the street this morning and I met Mrs. Nutting who asked me to go to ride with her today. I did not hardly want to go but I did. She said she was out of town Tuesday and that was the reason she did not come for me. We had a very nice drive. Ettie and a Miss Gray went with us. We went to Foster's Pond and to Rattlesnake Mountain. We had a lovely time but it was not a very pleasant afternoon. She asked me to come to her house to tea tomorrow to meet a Miss Eastman. She said she would come herself and ask Miss McKeen.

Recited to Miss Hall. Mrs. Nutting did come and saw Miss Brownell and Miss McK. let me go. I had a splendid time. Wore my white dress as it was warm. Lu Nutting is very nice. I went about half past five and came home about eight. Miss Eastman was there. She is quite a famous lecturer I think. I had a letter today. I did not expect to hear from her so soon.

Chapel at Abbot
Academy. Courtesy
Phillips Academy.

Went to Church as usual. Wrote Anna Hubbard today. I got permission to.

I wore my white dress to Church today. Spent my quarters with Mary Decker, Matie Kuhnen, Emma Tomey and Lillie Fahnestock.

This morning, I walked with Lily Fahnestock and this afternoon we went up to the grove and worked on fancy work awhile and then took a walk.

During study hours at five o'clock, Dr. and Mrs. Douglas called to see Annie Peabody and Lois Warner who go to the Episcopal Church. Miss B. asked me to go down too, so I went and had a pleasant call. I told Dr. D. that I had a letter of introduction to him from Dr. Carleton.

This morning we got the news that the president died last night. All the bells tolled here. Miss McKeen read all the particulars in the hall. We had been talking of having a picnic up to Sunset Rock and Miss B. thought it would be no harm to go. Sunset Rock is just as lovely as it can be and we had a grand time. We started about four and got home about seven.

This evening after half hours, Mary Hillard and Mary Gorton came up to our room.

Annie Peabody and I walked down street this afternoon. I bought starch, boot blacking and soap.

Hattie swept this a.m. and I studied my latin lesson and recited it at two. I also washed a few things.

Walked with Mary Decker and Lily Fahnestock. This afternoon Lois Warner went down street and I did not want to go so I went to walk with Hattie and Marion.

Walked with Mamie D. this A.M. and with Julia and Marion P.M. Tonight I was mourning because I did not have a letter from home when Mary Gorton came in with an express package from Papa. It was a big basket of grapes & a dozen bananas. Didn't I feel good.

Wrote to Louise today. We got to acting awfully in our Phys. Geog. class, Carrie Puffer, Miss Knevils, Miss Sanyea and myself.

Learned my lesson to recite to Miss Hall but I shall not recite it today as Miss Hall is away. Walked with Julia Spear A.M. and Hattie and I went down street P.M. A letter from Mother tonight.

Rather cloudy this A.M. before Church so I wore my thick dress but when we came from Church it was terribly warm so I put on my white dress. The minister preached about the president. The sermon was very good. After dinner, Miss B. read us about the funeral which is to be tomorrow. We had a hard time keeping cool this afternoon and all I did was to

Following page:
Ruth Anna Hatch's
class of 1885, Abbot
Academy. Courtesy
Phillips Academy.

131

lie down and eat grapes and bananas. Wrote to Grandma in the evening. Quarters with Julia Spear, Mamie D., Fanny French and Mary Bacon.

A very warm and uncomfortable day. It is Garfield's funeral day. There was no school till five tonight. We had a short exercise in the hall this morning and this afternoon we went down to the town hall for memorial services. Prof. Tucker delivered a splendid address and the great preacher Prof. Parke made the closing prayer. Nearly all the school wore black or white with a crape bar on the left shoulder. I wore white. Had only a postal from home tonight.

This P.M. Mary Gorton and I took a very long walk up to the old railroad and home over the hills. We did not get home till after five and when I did get home, Miss B. sent for me to come to her room. I found Miss Tappan there. She went off at six and I went down to the train to see her off. She is going out to Lawrence and she asked me to come out tomorrow morning to see her and I guess I shall go. Had a letter and answered it.

A very warm day. I started from here at nine and got to Lawrence in a few minutes. I had a splendid time. Miss Reed, Miss Tappan's friend has just got home from Europe & she showed us all her pictures. I got home just in time for dinner. This afternoon Annie Peabody and I went down street and got caught in a shower. I had my white dress on and it does not look very nice now. Mamie Duncombe does not study German so Miss McK. has moved her over to Smith Hall to make more room.

THURSDAY, SEPTEMBER 29, 1881

Walked this morning with Matie Kuhnen. P.M. with Lois Warner. We took a very long walk where we had never been before and got lost. We had a nice time. No letter today.

FRIDAY, SEPTEMBER 30, 1881

Mary Decker and I walked this morning. This afternoon, Marion Keene and I had a nice walk and then came back and ate under a tree and talked. It is very warm.

I had a correspondence card from Lizzie Chapman. Wrote to Papa tonight.

Very warm again.
Learned and recited
my latin lesson. Had
a splendid letter from
Anna Hubbard this
noon. Hattie and I
walked this afternoon
We went down street
and got some apples
and pickle limes.
In the study hour
Ellen brought me an
express box from Papa.
It was bananas and
a letter. I also had a
nice long letter from
home telling about
the dedication of the
Town hall. The letter had
a dollar in it.

SUNDAY, OCTOBER 2, 1881

Cloudy this morning
and a hard rain
some this evening.
Went to the Old
with as usual. Read
and all and lay down
this afternoon. Spent
awhile with Mary
...ton, Mattie Kuhnlen,
...ily Mather and
Marion Reuse.
...ve P. M. wrote a letter
...Josie Frich, but had
get special permission.

Very warm again. Learned and recited my Latin lesson. Had a splendid letter from Anna Hubbard this noon. Hattie and I walked this afternoon. We went down street and got some apples and pickle limes. In the study hour, Ellen brought me an express box from Papa. It was bananas and a letter. I also had a nice long letter from home telling about the dedication of the Town hall. The letter had a dollar in it.

Cloudy this morning and a hard rain storm this evening. Went to the Old South as usual. Read and ate and lay down this afternoon. Spent quarters with Mary Gorton, Matie Kuhnen, Emily Mather and Marion Keene.

This P.M. wrote a letter to Josie Fish, but had to get special permission.

Falmouth Town Hall, completed in 1881, as it was decorated for the bicentennial celebration in 1886. Courtesy WHHC.

A pouring rain storm this morning but nice and pleasant this afternoon. P.M. Lily Fahnestock a nice walk. Then I played on the piano and went to the Reading room and read awhile. Had a nice letter from Nellie tonight.

Studied and recited my lesson to Miss Hall. It is an awful feeling day. Everybody is complaining. Hattie and I walked a while but it was so hot we could not stand it long. I had a letter and a paper from Addie, and a letter from Papa with twenty postage stamps in it. I expect a box the first of next week.

Pleasant. I went to Church. Lay down most of the afternoon. Wrote to Ruth Basset. Spent quarters hours with Julia Spear, Lily Fahnestock and Annie Peabody. I could not report any sermon today as usual, so Miss B. told me I must report some next week.

Went to Miss McK. this morning to ask if I could not write to anybody I want to on Sunday. Of course she said no. *

* This sad comment is the final entry in the diary.

Abbot Female Academy.

THIS CERTIFIES THAT

Ruth Anna Hatch.

has honorably completed the prescribed course of Study at the ((**Abbot Female Academy**)) and by her attainments and correct deportment is entitled to this

TESTIMONIAL.

Given at ANDOVER this ninth day of June in the year of our Lord, one thousand eight hundred and eighty-five.

Edwards A. Park, Prest of the Trustees.   Philena McKeen, Principal

Ruth Anna
Hatch's diploma
from Abbot
Female Academy,
June 9, 1885.
Courtesy WHHC.

Ruth Anna Hatch was graduated from Abbot Academy on June 9, 1885. After teaching for a few years, she married her childhood friend, Asa Frank Shiverick, on April 23, 1891. They moved to Chicago where Frank joined his uncles Charles and Frank Tobey in the furniture business. On April 22, 1892, Ruth and Frank's first son, Arthur, was born. A second son, Francis Tobey, was born on September 18, 1896.

Asa Frank Shiverick died in Chicago in 1930. Ruth Anna moved back to Woods Hole and died here in 1937. They are buried with their families in the churchyard of the Church of the Messiah in Woods Hole.